Entertaining Angels

Entertaining Angels

Compiled by
Geoffrey Duncan

CANTERBURY
PRESS
Norwich

© In this compilation Geoffrey Duncan 2005

First published in 2005 by the Canterbury Press Norwich
(a publishing imprint of Hymns Ancient & Modern Limited,
a registered charity)
9–17 St Albans Place, London N1 0NX

www.scm-canterburypress.co.uk

British Library Cataloguing in Publication data

A catalogue record for this book is available
from the British Library

ISBN 1-85311-642-4

Typeset by Regent Typesetting, London
Printed and bound in Great Britain by William Clowes Ltd, Beccles, Suffolk

Contents

v

vi

Dedication

Asha,
this anthology is dedicated to you
as you grow up in a world in need of compassion and
hope.
Always look for the best in humankind . . .
watch for the good things that people bring to life.

Also, it is dedicated to the many women, men and
children who live in fear of persecution. Continue with
your determination for a better way of living as you
search for compassionate people who will help you in
your need. Always look for the hopeful signs and be
encouraged by people who will give you guidance . . .

. . . and not least, to the many people known and
unknown to each other . . .
go on . . .
and on . . .
and on . . .

entertaining angels.

Introduction

When *Entertaining Angels* was considered for publication there was a sense of urgency to provide new, stimulating material for the many worshipping communities around the world who aim to be alongside people in desperate need of compassion, love and care. The urgency is even greater now as western global societies and local communities appear to lack understanding and compassion for women, children and men in acute distress. Our global neighbours are refugees and asylum seekers, people held in detention, the homeless, the travellers, the lonely, single parents, the imprisoned, the many men and women who remain marginalized because of their sexuality, and many other people, each of whom is precious, in the sight of God and the love of Jesus Christ. I am sure we need in our churches, in society as a whole, to have far higher regard for humankind, for people in all their flesh and blood, hurt and agony, joy and sadness, laughter and tears, the tortured and the humiliated.

At this time there are Zimbabwean women who have been raped and tortured, yet governments do not regard rape as torture and are returning these defenceless women to that country. There are times when babies born to asylum seekers are taken away from their mother and placed in care. Innocent Afghanis are being deported to their country where Christians can face death. The credibility of converts to Christianity, especially people from Iran, is considered to be suspect and their words doubted as are the words of the people who support them.

Day by day homeless people are abused on the streets of towns and cities.

Repeatedly we learn of continued discrimination against men and women whose sexuality may or may not be different to ours. Basic human rights are denied to many people in our global situation.

I believe we should ask the question: 'Our God, Our God why have we forsaken them?'

It is time to be alongside, to walk with the many people whose lives have been developed in a different and colourful culture. Bring joy, peace and laughter into their lives. Appreciate their cultures and different ways of living. Restore their dignity. Women, men, children – all have a right to be respected, to be cared for, to receive hospitality, a friendly and non-patronizing word, help with no strings attached.

It is then that we shall learn the joy of living in a multi-cultural society and how these people enrich our lives.

Now, right now, is the time for a change of heart, a time to be joyful and 'entertain angels unawares' (Hebrews 13.2b). It is time to sing a new song to the Lord, especially as there are plenty of marvellous deeds waiting to be done.

Geoffrey Duncan
April 2005

During my daily spread of the most interesting responsibilities there is contact with many people and organizations who are at the forefront of aid, help and assistance. Please do get in touch via The Canterbury Press in case I may be able to help or point you in the direction of someone who will be able to do so.

1

Welcoming the Stranger

Do not neglect to show hospitality to strangers, for by doing that, some have entertained angels without knowing it.

Hebrews 13.2

A kind word and a welcoming smile will make a stranger from another land or even from around the corner feel that life is worthwhile. A senior citizen may feel neglected, a person may live with an impairment and need assistance with no strings attached, the elderly man or woman with advancing age and illness is in need of love, care and someone who will listen . . . We live in a time when people of different ages, cultures, race and faith need to know that there are people who will listen and comfort them.

The prayers and readings in this chapter will help us celebrate the richness of humankind.

As Duncan L. Tuck writes, 'You are Welcome' (page 3).

Welcome, Stranger!

Welcome, Stranger!
Place your palm
against my own.

Let us interlace
our fingers.

Then together
we will weave
the threads of our lives
into a wondrous vision;
a bright new
tapestry of dreams,
of times to come.

Susan Hardwick
England

You Are Welcome

In the name of the one
who was hated by many
and betrayed by his friends,
we welcome you.
  Here you may pause in your travels,
  safe from the darkness.

By the power of the one
who lived in weakness
and had no soft bed to lay in,
we open our home.
  Here you may rest from your troubles
  and soothe your sores.

3

Through the love of the one
who cared for all who came
and yet was rejected by society,
we accept you as you are.
Here you may lay down your defences
and be yourself.

For we do not understand.
We have not suffered as you,
but our Lord has,
and as we try to be his giving,
loving, sacrificial body,
so we share his concern.

Duncan L. Tuck
England

Lift Up the Other

To be at peace, let us respect one another.
The only time we must look down on someone
Is when we bend down to lift up the other.
Amen

Writer Unknown
A sister from the African Continent

On Being an Angel

I had intended to attend Eucharist that lunchtime but felt for
some odd reason that I should go to Mount Stuart Square in
Butetown, Cardiff, Wales. There I met briefly with one or two
friends and talked for a while but felt that I should stay and
walk around. I didn't know why!

Much to my surprise, a young fifteen-year-old Iranian girl
came up behind me, accompanied by her mother and asked
very politely for the way to the Citizens Advice Bureau in the

4

centre of Cardiff. They both looked tired and desperate. They had spent all morning walking from one solicitor's office to another asking for help with the mother's appeal for asylum. Following several miles of walking and blunt rejections, both of them, as devout Muslims, prayed that God would send them an angel. They got me instead!

Fortunately, a colleague of mine was in her office and able to help. For a while, my friend and I listened to the story of what happens to fifteen-year-old girls when they have to cope with fleeing their country, settle in a new environment and act as translators and solicitors for their families. After phoning around, a solicitor in Cardiff was found who was willing to listen to their story. I took them to visit him. After studying the papers overnight he felt that there were grounds for appeal and lodged the papers the following day.

As tough as things are for displaced people, dare I suggest that someone is on their side. I have had the thrill of being many things over the years but none of them will ever beat being an angel.

Aled Edwards
Wales

Yusuf, Yitzak and John

They came, these wise men,
alone in their loneliness
each drawn by Love –
the only Star that shone
in the kingdom of their hearts,
a Star leading them
to gift themselves
to the image of Christ
in the hungry and thirsty
in the face of the stranger
in the shame of the naked
in the sick and imprisoned.

And in gifting themselves
in compassion to these
they found their togetherness
and returned to their homes
celebrating their belonging
to the kingdom of God.

Harry Wiggett
South Africa

They Came to Tea

They came to tea.
We shared food and conversation together
and caught a glimpse of the
Love of God.

They shared stories of their lives.
We listened to each other
and learned anew of the
Compassion of Christ.

They presented a challenge.
We talked about ways of living together
and came near the reconciling
Spirit of Justice, Joy and Peace.

Let us celebrate and share
love, compassion and justice.

Geoffrey Duncan
England

The Invitation

It was just a simple meal,
But more –
An invitation
To share in life
And love.

It was a simple meal,
But it was more –
Your wanting and caring,
Your sharing

Time together,
Warmth,
Conversation,
About nothing,
And everything . . .

It was just a simple meal,
But more –
It was enough – a feast.

Claire Smith
Guyana

Emmaus Walk

'Don't talk to strangers,' we are
Told in childhood. It takes years
To grow through infant training.
Daring to trust comes with maturity,
Or perhaps is born of desperation.
The Emmaus two discovered
That the stranger unlocked
Understanding;
Shared food became a blessing.

Ann Lewin
England

Call No One Stranger
This poem can be read by many different voices

You first saw them by the roadside
    standing at the crossroads, waiting . . .
    listening . . . watching

They walked in silence, small bundles on their backs
        clutching other bits in their hands.
Fear on the faces of those women, men and children.
Frightened by the past, fearful of the future
Will no one understand their pain?
Will anyone open a door to receive them?
Look again and you will see
        familiar people . . .
        mothers and fathers,
        sisters and brothers,
        grandparents.
Listen and you will hear
        familiar sounds . . .
        talking, crying, laughing.
Understand and you will know
        the stuff of which your dreams are made . . .
        love and laughter, security and safety,
        peace and prosperity . . .
        are their dreams too.
That which is joy to every human heart
        is not alien to theirs
The peace you long for is that same peace
        they strive for.
We stand together as one . . .
        drawing warmth from the same sun and
        life from the same earth
And though we travel on different roads
We're part of one God, one Earth, one Universe . . .
There are no strangers.
Tears shed in compassion . . .
        songs of love and dreams of peace
        make us all one.
Recognise your family in the stranger
Open your door, invite them in
        to sit at your table
        and share your bread.
Call no one stranger

whose roots are kin to your own . . .
whose lives all spring from the
One Great Fountain of Life!

Patricia Mulhall, CAFOD
England

Strangers and Angels

A dialogue between ourselves and our consciences, for two voices, plus a voice from the body of the church/meeting place to read the introductory verses from Hebrews 13.2–3, GNB:

'Remember to welcome strangers into your homes. There are some who did that, and welcomed angels without knowing it.'

Voice 1 What do you mean by strangers?

Voice 2 People we don't know. People who may be different or unusual.

Voice 1 It's easier to talk to people I know.

Voice 2 But they were strangers once.

Voice 1 Some people are easy to get to know and to make friends with.

Voice 2 You mean because they are like you and you have common interests, but couldn't that be a bit blinkered? You may be missing out on some very interesting people.

Voice 1 But they wouldn't think the same as me, they may have different ideas, customs and moral values, and, they might not even believe in the same things I believe in.

Voice 2 Exactly!

Voice 1 I suppose Jesus welcomed some strange people.

9

Voice 2 Yes. Jesus welcomed all kinds of people and found in them qualities that others couldn't see. And they found in him God's unconditional love for everyone.

Voice 1 I see. So, what is an angel?

Voice 2 A messenger from God

Voice 1 Are you saying that these 'strangers' could be able to tell me things about God that I don't know?

Voice 2 If you get to know them and welcome them, then yes that could well be so. But, be prepared – they may be more like angels than we are.

Voice 1 Jesus came as a stranger and a messenger from God, too.

Voice 2 Exactly! And some welcomed him and some despised and rejected him.

Voice 1 Because they didn't recognise him.

Voice 2 Do we always recognise him? Remember, he said 'I was a stranger and you wouldn't welcome me into your homes.'

Voice 1 Then he said, 'Whenever you refused to help one of those least important ones, you refused to help me.'

Voice 2 Yes. But they weren't least important in his eyes, only in ours. For 'least important' think 'marginalised'.

Voice 1 I've got some serious thinking to do.

Heather Johnston
Scotland

Entertaining an Angel Unawares

I remember that day
so very well,
the day I entertained

an angel unaware.
Late one night,
a knock at the door –
the homeless, raggedy man
who stood there.
A private sigh,
a forced, public smile,
the door held wide
and a 'do come in'.
The teacup gratefully cradled,
the food sandwiching the words:
'Yes, I've come a long way.'
The voice so soft
yet strong,
the gaze so piercing
yet pure.
Then he stood so tall,
lightly touched my arm –
and how his touch did burn! –
'Thank you!'
spoken so tenderly,
the blessing caressing
and encircling my soul.
'Who *are* you?'
I whispered,
as he disappeared from view.
But in reality I knew –
as I have since always known
for sure –
that day,
that night,
I had entertained
an angel
unawares.

Susan Hardwick
England

Meeting and Eating

Henges[1] were spaces and places
where Ancients were meeting and eating.
They'd take off the turf,
pile up the earth,
and party for all they were worth.

Churches are spaces and places
for contemporary meeting and eating.
So get off your seat,
wash your neighbour's feet
and make sure there's plenty to eat.

Janet Lees
England

Let's Have a Meal, Let's Have a Feast!

Let's have a meal, let's have a feast!
  Come one and all, from great to least:
the food and drink have been prepared,
  the Lord provides, and all is shared.

Let's have a meal, let's have a feast!
  This table cannot be policed:
it's not the church's, it's the Lord's,
  it's spread for free, not for reward.

Let's have a meal, let's have a feast!
  From 'us' and 'them' we've been released:
no strangers here, for all are friends,
  no need to hide, deride, defend.

---

[1] Henges are found throughout Britain: of prehistoric construction they are all characterised by banks and ditches of earth surrounding a large enclosed space, the most famous of which is Stonehenge in Wiltshire.

Let's have a meal, let's have a feast!
  Join hearts and hands, and pass the peace:
Christ turned the cheek and walked the mile,
  now all to each are reconciled.

Let's have a meal, let's have a feast!
  Let grace abound, let joy increase!
And as we take the bread and wine,
  let who we are be re-defined.

Tune: Truro

Kim Fabricius
Wales/USA

Bless the Lord for Your Coming

The Lord bless your smile –
The unexpected welcome.
The Lord bless your hands –
Worn with your own cares but swiftly open to mine.
The Lord bless you for following your path when it was right
  that ours should cross.

I know not your name,
but I bless the Lord for your coming at the moment of my
  greatest need.
You are the angel born of my frailty; the light at the end of
  my strength;
And though I may never see you again (for it is a vast and
  fascinating world),
still I leave you the richer, and I pray that something of our
  meeting will pull our
shores so close, others may cross in future without fear.

Duncan L. Tuck
England

Reaching Out

When you are talking
to a really old person
they seem to only
half hear and see you.

They look at you
as if you are just an outline of a person
that hasn't been filled in
and they only reply to your words
that have specific meaning to them.

And sometimes when you are leaving
they reach out and
grasp your hand or wrist really tightly
and hang on as if to something precious.
Then let go and sit back
eyes closed, worn out by the effort.

Jayne Greathead
England

Sheltering God

Sheltering God,
You were born in flight,
Your parents anxious and given no rest.
The manner of your birth calls me to
Open-heartedness and sensitivity to the strangers in our midst.
Help me not to flee your challenge.
The violence of the present time teaches me fear of the stranger,
Reluctant to reach out to those who are different.
Grace me this day as I seek
To see you in the faces of those uprooted,
Weary, as they seek refuge and peace.
Amen.

Jane Deren
USA

Loving God

Loving God
we are all your family;
united in our devotion to you
and our care for others.
Help us to reflect that love
through the life of the churches,
so that people may know
that yours is a warm-hearted and open family,
ready to welcome anyone
who needs your care.
Teach us to love as Jesus did –
with open-hearted warmth
towards the most unexpected people.

Marjorie Dobson
England

Jesus, Friend and Brother

You know what it is like
To be hungry and thirsty.

You know the plight of the
Stranger who is made unwelcome.

You know the suffering of all
Who have lost everything.

We pray that by welcoming
The asylum seeker we may show
Love for our neighbour and
Draw closer to you.
Amen.

Tony Singleton / CAFOD
England

Here Was a Man

Haunted
He stumbled in, hung a moment
Wing-spread in our darkness,
Having nipped down our back alley-way,
His best Oxfam suit a misfit
With its pin stripes looking for some lamppost to lean on.

I'd seen pictures like. Who hadn't?
But they're always smaller – they always are.

You could see it was all too much –
Carried it in the eyes.
The commotion out front was slowly hammering
His head lower and lower. Piercing. All shared out,
His worldly goods no longer baggage
We sat, quiet like,
Him clutching a cup of tea
Yet somehow, holding me.
Cavernous; a silence multiplying everything
Out of nothing; food for all.

> *Here was a man who could turn the world around,*
> *I thought.*

I squeezed another cup of tea from the pot,
Knowing sooner or later
Crowds would carry Him off.

Eve Jackson
England

Beware Hasty Assumptions

A knock at the door caught us by surprise. The woman
standing there asked for a chair. 'I'm sorry to trouble you,' she
thoughtfully said, 'but my husband has broken his leg.'

A friend who'd just arrived for lunch after a lengthy journey
appeared as baffled as I was. She read my thoughts exactly: if

a broken leg was suspected, an ambulance – not a chair – was needed. Fortunately we recognised this was no time to argue and soon realised we'd made hasty assumptions that, in this instance, were quite inappropriate. Seeing Peter sat on the front lawn, trying to fix a broken clip, the unfamiliar complications of the situation suddenly dawned on us. For this was no ordinary 'broken' leg of flesh and bone but an artificial limb!

My friend, whose car was parked on the road outside, immediately offered the traumatised couple a lift back to their home – a short distance away.

Delia and I had planned our day together some weeks in advance but the timing was perfect. As I'm not a car driver, I could only stand and wait for her to come to the rescue but I was given the opportunity to get to know two more of our neighbours – both extremely grateful for their lift home.

Wendy Whitehead
England

Inn Signs

There were two innkeepers.
Do you blame him, that first one,
For only offering an outhouse?
It was a busy time –
You know the pressures –
Important visitors arriving –
What else could he do?
He did at least make room.

The other, hardly notices,
Might have opened his door
To real trouble, letting that
Good Samaritan drag him in.
Who else lurked in the shadows?
Quite a risk, getting involved.

Both offered space –
And life began to grow.
Were both inns called
The Birth of Hope?

Ann Lewin
England

Responding to Small Miracles

My God,
is she not a miracle?
You brought her to existence
through all the trials
of sperm wars and fallopian tubes,
through nine months of fragile growth,
and here she is – unique.
Only a small person
amongst jostling billions
on your beautiful planet,
yet (the perfect wonder)
you love her.
Not Caucasian,
not white, Anglo-Saxon,
no privileges of sanitation
and political stability;
but you name her your child.
No access to health care,
computers, holidays,
or a balanced diet;
still you are by her side.
So when she enters my world,
brought in by parents
seeking sanctuary and dreams,
can I see her as you do
and let my life respond
to your small miracles?

Duncan L. Tuck
England

18

Is it Nothing to You?

Nothing? No, far from it!
We all had felt the tugging of those eyes
upon the skirt folds of our Christian consciences.

Silent and motionless each day he sat, against the wool shop
    wall.
Above his head, mid-seasonal reductions,
pullovers and fleecy coats, tartan scarves and gloves,
in glowing autumn purples, browns and golds,
to keep at bay the chill November wind
which this year took us so much by surprise –
just as he had.

Blown in from where, we wondered?
What was the claim upon us of those eyes, since there he
    chose to sit,
asking for nothing at all? Somehow they called for a
    response,
though what it was we did not know for sure.

Nothing? No, far from it!
Searching our repertoire of empathy, we did our best.

A triangle of sandwiches from Boots – the best they say, won
    an award this year.
In there this morning, I was buying toothpaste –
three for the price of two, this week.

A coffee from Macdonald's – mind, it's hot!
I'll leave it here beside you on the ground.
Must hurry now, I see my bus is coming in.

Do you need money (pity)? Shall we call the Nightstop
    people?
You need a social worker? Doctor? Priest?
Or all of these – or none? Perhaps you're 'happy as you are'?

The Salvation Army, now – they'll know what to do.
We are running out of ideas.

No longer there against the wool shop wall,
somehow his huddled form is squatting in the shadows still
which day by day grow deeper now, as Christmas lights
ever more brightly call us to the urgent task
of shopping for the festive season –

all we who pass by.

Gillian Collins
England

Each Person Is God's Image

Each person is God's image
and thus inviolable
in body, mind and spirit.
Consequently
every offence against another person
in word or action
is a burglary
into the most righteous and most vulnerable
living-space of life,
where the fragile child of the divine self-respect
is born, is raised and gets its nutriment.

Each person is equal to any other person.
No one is superior,
no one subordinate.
All have an equal value.
Consequently
every offence against another person
is a crime,
an abuse of power,
that injures not only a single person,
but the whole of humanity.

Per Harling
Sweden

Angel on Call

Let me introduce . . .
an angel I know well.

Far from any likeness
to some ethereal being,
she's an essentially practical,
down-to-earth companion.

Constantly on call,
far-sighted and alert,
ready to console, cajole or guide,
it's always reassuring to confide in her.

She watches, listens,
jogs my memory –
stirs me and others, toward prayer,
united action or use of hidden talent.

Signalling diverse human need
waiting to be assessed and met,
wherever it exists,
I'm reminded often of all who respond
to nudges from this guardian angel
to celebrate community.

Wendy Whitehead
England

From the Unborn Child to His Father

Be there.
Remember that I have two parents.
It's got to be unconditional love.
Teach.
Enjoy our time.

Set boundaries, but remember I'm a child.
Let me learn by the example you set.
Never hit. Try not to shout or lose your temper.

Dave
England

Exchange

It's Friday, about 3.30 in the afternoon.
My phone goes.
It's my eldest, Ben.
'What you up to, Dad?'
'Nothing much!'
'Well, I've just finished my first week at work and
I thought we could go for a pint.'

He's in the beer garden waiting.
'I'll get these,' I say,
'No, Dad, I'll get them in.'
'Yeah, OK. Cheers, son.'
'Cheers, Dad. How was your day?'

Adam
England

The Single Prayer

To those far away
Strangers I shall never meet,
I wrap my thoughts in a prayer.

Cradled between solemn promises
and wishful dreams
are Words of Peace.

My single prayer; a lingua franca
amidst a chorus of new morning
everywhere.

Layers of hope, doubt,
hope, may fall away
like tiny distractions,

but in the reaching out
strands of love will unravel,
from hand to helping hand, hearts

to mind. Drawing the circle
ever closer. The space between
changing, as the act of unwrapping

re-shapes every one of us
until Peace is born
of us all.

Eve Jackson
England

Drive out the Prejudices

Lord, drive out the prejudices that make me judge without
experience, the complacency that will not recognise the good
in what is alien to me.

Give me the grace to find you in unlikely people and unexpected
places and to look always with the open eyes of faith and not
with the half-closed eyes of fixed opinion.

Lord of love, when the outward sight looks on another's need,
give the inward sight which sees that all humanity is one in
Christ and responds even against personal inclination and
selfishness. When I say that everyone is my neighbour as a
child of God, let it not be a pious word without feeling but a
truth that reaches into the depth of my being and out into the
world where the journeys of so many are lonely and perilous.

Raymond Chapman
England

Doors

Doors open and close
lockless free-swinging
locked when knocked upon
some labelled alas
for particular persons.
Innumerable the doors
through which men pass
but one alone is yours
is yours alone controlled
its fabric not the oak
of acorns growing –
the handle key the lock
the knock of flesh and blood
your heart
which you alone can open.

Harry Wiggett
South Africa

Alem

Alem prays in a way that is different.
She stands after Mass with her hands held high
And bows her head three times in worship.

On her forehead is a painted cross
With a smaller cross high on both her cheeks.
She originally lived in Ethiopia.

Twenty years ago she left for Arabia
Where it was hard to buy food in the market
With the marks of a Christian,

So she came to London with two young children.
Alone and frightened, she was helped by my church.
Here she is cared for, respected, much loved.

The most important truth she has shown me
Is to be myself as she is herself.

It doesn't matter that speech can be difficult.
What effort have I made to try to learn Tigri?

Alem prays in a way that is different
And that has an impact beyond any words.

Sarah Ingle
England

Beyond

Parent God, help us to see as you see,
beyond the labels that make people strangers.
Beyond the disability,
beyond the illness,
beyond pain,
to the gift of diversity in the people you have made.

Brother God, help us to see as you see,
beyond the labels that make people strangers.
Beyond the sexuality,
beyond the lifestyle,
beyond the gender,
to the gift of diversity in the people you have made.

Spirit God, help us to see as you see,
beyond the labels that make people strangers.
Beyond the fashion statement,
beyond the qualifications,
beyond the lack of qualifications,
to the gift of diversity in the people you have made.

Creator God, help us to see as you see,
beyond the immediate.

25

Beyond the buildings to your wonderful sky,
beyond the supermarket shelf to field and farmer,
beyond the organisation to community,
to the gift of unity in your world.

Human God, help us to see as you see,
beyond the immediate.
Beyond the hungry face,
beyond the refugee status,
beyond the poverty,
to the gift of unity in your world.

Inspiring God, help us to see as you see,
beyond the immediate.
Beyond the politics of party,
beyond the headlines in the media,
beyond the divisions in society,
to the gift of unity in your world.

John Ll. Humphreys
Scotland/Wales

Let the Little Children

'Is Bob there?' asks the child on our doorstep, clutching what was once a bicycle. 'Can he mend this?' I am doubtful, but pretty soon there's a full-blown informal community bicycle repair workshop going on outside our back door. Two more broken machines have appeared and children call to each other in Punjabi and English. 'What's happening?' More and more flock to join asking, 'What's this for, Bob?' and 'Is this it?' as they search for spare parts in an unlikely pile of scrap. He shows them how to put a puncture patch on and then everyone wants a go. Once the tyre is fixed and it's time to inflate it, it's all hands to the pump, literally. Everyone takes a turn while Bob looks for a screw or nut that might just hold the saddle on or the brake blocks in place. Everyone is chatting together and trying to co-operate. News is exchanged and a few chappatis passed around. Eventually the bicycles are declared fit for service or at least as good as they can be for now and everyone departs shouting 'Bye' and 'Thanks' in various languages. It seems to me as I watch it all, that if Jesus lived in Firth Park* he would mend bicycles.

Janet Lees
England

* Firth Park, Sheffield, UK

My Church – A Bridge for the Stranger

Leader: We are here to listen and to learn
– along with all women and men –
from stories
from situations
from facts and figures
from the voices of people
that cry out for our
attention.

People: Forgive us, God of all People, for those times when we have chosen not to listen to the voices of women and men and chosen not to listen to their stories.

Leader: We hear the cries of the people – their cries for dignity, hope, justice and freedom to be.

People: Forgive us as we, the Church, through our inattention and our fears, have added to their pain and despair of being strangers in an unknown land.

Leader: When people feel demoralised and desperately afraid through lack of support.

People: Give us the courage to speak out for them and to give them strength to plead for their rights.

Leader: When hopelessness drowns their dreams and loneliness is their only companion.

People: May we affirm to those with power and authority the right of women and men to be who they are and to give hope and warmth to these people in their desperate situations.

Leader: God of all People, empower the Church – the people of God –

> to hear
>> to listen
>>> to act

and to take risks to be the voice of those people whose voices are overpowered by the clamour and hypocrisy of the world around them.

Silence

People: Loving God, who calls the Church – the people of God – to be the

> **Church of the Stranger**
>> **Enable us to hear**
>>> **Enable us to listen**
>>>> **Empower us to act.**

Geoffrey Duncan
England

Open Door

Who is the stranger at the door,
travel-stained, exhausted,
looking for a place to stay?
Tension is etched into her face,
haunting memories of a shattered home,
of relatives and friends slaughtered.
Come in and welcome;
Let us share together.

Who is the stranger at the door,
knocking without much hope,
yet desperate to enter?
He has been broken by prison,
spent months in solitude
and fears for his life if he returns.
Come in and welcome;
Let us journey together.

Who is the stranger at the door,
marks of blood on his forehead
and scars on his hands?
His face is somehow familiar;
his eyes reflect sadness,
yet his lips convey a smile.
Come in and welcome;
Let us go forward together.

John Johansen-Berg
England

Torn

I want to make them welcome,
But they do not speak our tongue,
They have so many children –
Hungry, weary and so young;
I want to make them welcome
But I'm frightened they will take
The substance of our being
That we've worked so hard to make . . .
They have so many children,
Hungry, weary and so young –
I want to make them welcome . . .

But I do not speak their tongue.

Margot Arthurton
England

Solitude

Just when I get a moment to myself
the phone rings
and I hear the voice
I know so well.
I also know
that time will soon be flying.

But loneliness,
not an issue for me,
is hard for her –
and keeping me a little longer
on the line
puts off the moment
of the single cup of tea
and listless
staring at the television set.

Solitude is not a state
wished for by everyone.

Marjorie Dobson
England

I Vow to Love My Neighbour

I vow to love my neighbour, whatever race or creed,
to join her in her suffering, to plead with him in need.
This love will always question, will search out right and
    wrong,
will give itself for justice, for those who don't belong.
This love will never falter, till every soul is free,
till nations held in bondage can sing of liberty.

Through scenes of devastation, through famine, drought and
    war,
we'll work in ways of gentleness, work hard till we restore
the vision of the people, the hope of human grace,
till nations dwell in peacefulness together in this place;
till all the world together can sing in joyful praise
till all have found communion together in our days.

Andrew Pratt
England

Mistaken Identity
(a reflection on human relationships)

You come into view,
indistinctly as yet . . .
Through the mist I see
your outstretched arm.
What are you holding?
I feel uneasy,
fearful of your intentions . . .
Is that a weapon in your hand?

You are a threat, a danger,
Unknown, untrusted, unwanted . . .
Your approach unsettles me.
Come no nearer – or I'll . . .

You do not stop . . .
And something holds me there.
Now you have come more clearly into sight,
arm still outstretched
and holding – not a weapon
– but a gift! –

Friend, you break through
the barrier of my fear,
changing my perspective
by the courage of your love.

Wendy Ross-Barker
England

Souvenir

Every third Sunday we have her out
to give her a bit of family life.
At ninety she is as fragile as edelweiss,
like a small, white, alpine flower.
This is her favourite tune and
Norman who does the old dears disco
has made her an audio tape.

Sometimes we sit on the sofa
and watch *The Sound of Music*
just so that she can see it sung.
I try to hide the lump in my throat.

We cherish her like best china
feed her soft food:
doll-sized sandwiches, sponge cake,
two spoons of ice-cream.
She balances her plate daintily,
admires the pretty paper napkins;
the tulip tablecloth which used to be hers.

Today she talks about the war with Saddam;
knows more on that score than we do –
facts absorbed from the twenty-four hour beast
which squats in the corner of the lounge
at the home where she lives.

When I tell her that the average age
of the sailors on the *Ark Royal* is twenty-five
she gasps in disbelief, remembering how her
own husband's ship was blown to bits . . .

After six when she has trilled along
with *Songs of Praise* for long enough,
reminiscent of church choir days,
we take her back.

She always says
Thank you for the nice day
As I press a goodies bag into her hands:
soap, tissues, a few sweets –
and a clean, pretty paper napkin
like the one she has used at tea.

Denise Bennett
England

Receiving Jesus

Two friends of mine from my local church are authorised to take
Holy Communion to the sick and housebound of the parish.
Recently, they told me a story of a visit to one of the elderly
people on their list: Thomasina, always called 'Tommy'. Visiting
Tommy can sometimes be a bit of an ordeal, because Tommy is
rather deaf and often confused, although she is always pleased
to have visitors. She is a lonely woman, a widow for many years,
and lives in a tiny, somewhat run-down flat. On this occasion,
the conversation went like this:

'Hello Tommy, it's Jane and Margaret. We've brought you
Holy Communion.'
'Eh? What? You've brought what?'
'Holy Communion, Tommy. From church.'
'I don't know anything about that.'

'We've brought you the Bread, Tommy, OK?'
'Bread? Is that all you've got, bread? I've got some cheese . . .
and soup . . . and . . .'
'No Tommy, you don't understand – we've brought Jesus!'
'Jesus? You've brought Jesus!??'
'Yes Tommy.'
'Well, don't just stand there! If you've brought Jesus, take him
in the kitchen, and give him a cup of tea and a bit of supper!
I'll be in to see him when I've done me hair!'

We all laughed when we heard this story, but on reflection I
have found it both thought-provoking and remarkable. Two
thousand-odd years ago, Jesus sat down with his disciples at a
meal and made their special celebration into the ritual of his life
and death that would enter their (and our) memory. Christians
in so many different traditions do this in memory of him and
we who share Holy Communion together become by exten-
sion, members of that discipleship around that table. We go to
be fed – and we are fed. The trouble is, we are happy to forget everything *else* that went on at that extraordinary occasion.
John says Jesus washed his disciples' feet and asked them to
serve others in the same way – do we do *this* in memory of him?
In Luke, Jesus says 'the greatest among you must become like
the youngest, and the leader like one who serves'. Do we do *this*
in memory of him?

What I love about this story of Tommy, is her instinctive welcome and hospitality. If her friends have only bread, then she
will find fish to share. If Jesus should, amazingly, have come to
dine with her, as once he did with outcasts and sinners, then of
course he must be hungry and thirsty. He must be given food
and drink while she made an effort to look nice to welcome
him. It is as if she has John 13.20 written in her heart: 'whoever
receives one whom I send receives me and whoever receives
me receives him who sent me'. And if a lonely, housebound and
elderly lady can think instinctively not of herself but of others,
then why can't we, who are also of the Christian fellowship, the
Body of Christ?

When we meet the stranger, the deprived ones, the lost and

the lonely, no less than the widow, the orphan, or simply, in these days, the neighbour we never speak to, will we meet Christ in them, serve rather than be served? Or must Jesus forever stand and knock at the locked doors of our faith?

Anne Richards
England

Love Is Made the Way You Want it to Be

What is love?
Love is what I would call trust
You need to trust someone before you
Can love them.
I was in love once and I'm still in love
Now
I trust this person with all my heart
He's like my best friend and also
Like my diary he keeps all my secrets
safe.

Why do people fall in love?
People fall in love because they
Are attracted to the way people are
Physically and mentally.
When I fell in love for the first time
I loved him because of what he was.
But later on in life I learned
To love him for who he was not what he
was.

How is love made?
Love is made the way you want it to be
So if you really love someone make
It last a lifetime because it may not
come again.

Zola F.
England

Incomer

Who is this man
What does he want of us –
New life and hope here . . .
And peace?
Do we have peace?
What can we give?
Do we have work –
Will he shirk,
Or take all our jobs
And outshine us?

What shrine does he seek,
What promised land –
Freedom, or free money,
Land of milk and honey maybe?
But see –
We have but scant ourselves –
Too little work,
Too few homes,
And many troubles . . .

How can we welcome him,
Make him at home,
Share our lot with him,
When barely can we quite sustain
Ourselves –

We cannot
For the inn in our minds is full.

Margot Arthurton
England

Loving a Neighbour
(based on the Story of the Good Samaritan)

I was riding confidently
On the road to Jericho,
When masked men appeared suddenly
And roped me around my torso –
From my donkey I was pulled down
And pinned by two husky men to the ground.

I wanted to shout
but my face was slapped
and a heavy hand was pressed to my mouth.
My golden necklace was yanked,
Leaving a gash on my neck.
Then they took all my shekels and hit me till I was a wreck.

Numb from head to foot,
I couldn't see and could barely hear
The eerie distant sound of an owl's hoot.
I told my self to be brave and be patient.
It will be a long dark night
But surely morning will come and there'll be light.

I was barely conscious
But could take stock of my life.
I counted the times I have been vicious
To people, including my children and my wife.
It is part of life's tragicomedy,
That one does things for which he will be sorry.

I will try to change
I told myself. I will amend.
I will have a new life in exchange
For a rescue from my present predicament.
I will relate to all in a new way
I promised God before the dawning of the new day.

37

Loud steps awakened me
I could barely open my eyes
But from afar I could easily recognise
The man on the donkey is a temple priest
A man of God is coming!
I was grateful. Help, at long last, is in the offing.

My heart sunk very low –
For the man just gave me a quick glance
Then walked away hesitantly but slow.
It was obvious he didn't want to take the chance
To touch, or be seen with, a person dying,
Lest his action taint his sacrificial offering.

As a child I went to the temple.
I remember how the priests exhorted the people
'To love Yahweh and do great a favour
by loving, as yourself, your neighbour.'
The law must be practised daily
For the prophets taught that religion is one with morality.

If only people listen to the prophets,
I would not be in this horrible situation.
They taught about love and justice,
About righteousness and compassion,
That religious sacrifices are less important
Than life overflowing with justice and love abundant!

I was about to faint again
When I noticed a Levite was approaching.
The young Levite would ease my pain
And he will help me out of my suffering.
Oh, no! He is also going away –
Why, temple people aren't supposed to act this way!

O men of the temple,
Caretakers of Yahweh's tabernacle –
Listen to the groaning of oppressed people;
Lessen the pain and hardship of those who struggle.

There is more than just worship and ritual;
There are more pressing and greater needs than the
　spiritual!

The sun is now at its brightest;
Its searing heat is burning my face.
I am aching all over! Is this heaven's test?
Have I been so bad, have I been so base?
'Why should (I) die before my time?'[1]
God forbid! Without me, my wife and children will cling to
　a vine.

I wanted to go to sleep.
I have lost a lot of blood and I'm very weak.
Then I heard the sound of a horse's footsteps.
It would just be my luck if it were another priest.
Oh, no, this is even worse; it is a Samaritan!
He won't help and I wouldn't want to be touched by such a
　man.

Quickly he alighted from his beast
And walked toward where I rest.
So he would leave, I pretended to be dead.
Not to be deterred, he knelt and put his hand on my forehead.
He whispered to me not to worry;
That he will help and will deliver me from my misery.

Our people hate the Samaritans.
I learned this since I was a child.
But if you ask me, I do not really know why.
And how can I hate this man who has come to help me?
He seems sincere and has no qualms
About helping a dying Jew, gently stroking my head with
　his palms.

The Samaritan salved my wounds,
And washed the dirty dried blood on my face,
Then put me on his horse to the nearest inn.

---

[1] Ecclesiastes 7.17b

39

I heard him tell the innkeeper to take good care of me
And promised he will come back to pay for his service.
The innkeeper took him at his word – a man of honour he
    must be!

My experience taught me greatly,
About loving, instead of hating, an enemy.
Now I know the meaning of 'loving a neighbour as
    yourself'.[2]
The Samaritan by his action showed me!
I did not get to know him nor able to say 'Thank you.'
But I'm sure he'd say, 'I am deeply grateful for the chance to
    help you!'

'Love your neighbour' –
not an easy commandment to follow.
Who are the people I must regard as my neighbour?
For the Samaritan that is the wrong question.
How can I *be* a neighbour? That should be the intention.
The Samaritan taught me to *be*, not to *find*, a neighbour!

Salvador T. Martinez
Thailand

Blessed are . . .

Blessed are the wanderers and those adrift
Blessed are the strangers at our door
Blessed are the unfed, the homeless on the road
Blessed is the child crying in pain
Blessed is the mother looking frantically for her children
separated on the journey
Blessed are those who welcome Christ to be born again when
they welcome these lost ones
Blessed are we who struggle to make a place in our hearts for
all of our brothers and sisters.
Amen

Jane Deren
USA

---

[2] Leviticus 19.18

Move out – To Entertain

Loving God
    walk with us as we move out from our security
Compassionate Christ
    motivate us to take risks like Jesus
Spirit of God
    reassure
    renew
    and recommit us to a life of service
    with no strings attached
    where we will live for justice and peace.

Amen

Geoffrey Duncan
England

Little Flute

Your voice is my little flute.

When the world treats you unfairly,
An indignant penny whistle.

In pain, you wail like the siren
Of a tin police car.

In the playground you tweet
Nonsense and invective.
I've heard you.

But home together we make music.
Flute tells me his hopes.
Flute tells me his hurts and fears.

Flute tootles that he loves me.

His snore is the foghorn of a toy boat.

Chanting a hymn in the echoing loo,
Flute sounds like
An angel.

Lucy Berry
England

Ruth (1)

Today I look with love upon this child –
the baby that I never thought to bear –
and, when he hears the story of my life,
he'll know he owes his being to God's care.

Those days in Moab seem so long ago,
my family home a strange and distant place,
for I have learned to live in Bethlehem
and look with love into a foreign face.

I well remember when Naomi came.
Her husband and her sons were fit and strong
and I, a child from Moab, did not think
that I would be her daughter before long.

But, when her husband died, her sons were grown.
Orpah and I were chosen as their wives.
Ten happy years we had, until their deaths,
then we must make a choice about our lives.

We knew Naomi wanted to go back,
her faith and home had roots in Bethlehem
and we would travel with her, so we thought,
but she urged us to go back home again.

Orpah turned back, but I would never leave;
my future now was at Naomi's side.

Although I could not know that it would lead
to my becoming someone else's bride.

Those strange days when I gleaned the barley fields
were frightening, for I did not know how;
it was the wise advice Naomi gave
led me to Boaz, kinsman, and husband now.

Because I followed in Naomi's faith
I was accepted, both by God and man
and now, at last, I have a cherished son;
perhaps this always was part of God's plan.

So, when I cradle Obed in my arms,
touch his warm cheek and watch his sleeping face,
I thank God for the wisdom of his ways
for surely he has led me to this place.

Marjorie Dobson
England

Celebrate Each Difference

We cannot make an easy, safe distinction,
all people are our neighbours, none denied.
The voices of all nations heard beside us:
all sisters, brothers, none we should deride.

The wall between the peoples has been broken.
In love of God divisions disappear.
As seen in Christ, we recognise our neighbours.
We greet unusual faces without fear.

We celebrate each difference God has given.
Each nation, black and white, both straight and gay,
the able and the challenged, God has offered,
that we might share together, learn and pray.

43

We meet with those who paint a different picture,
who value God in words not yet our own.
In dialogue we offer one another
a vision we could never find alone.

This God we seek is greater than each difference;
the source and ground of all variety,
the centre and the soul of all creation,
erasing hate with love, to set us free.

Andrew Pratt
England

2

Hunger for Justice

For I was hungry and you gave me food,
I was thirsty and you gave me something to drink.
Matthew 25.35

Cry out for Justice and then we shall have Peace.

Clean water is of paramount importance. A child dies every fifteen seconds because of the lack of clean, pure water. People die from hunger in an age which is mainly affluent for many people in our societies. We must promote healthy living.

Here we meet a kaleidoscope of people, the senior citizens of the world, the women, men and children who live with HIV/AIDS which is an ever-increasing illness of the twenty-first century, the people who wonder how they will gain access to public buildings and transport, the Dalit women who crush boulders to provide small stones for a road surface, children who scavenge on garbage dumps, exploited tea-pickers, exploited sugar farmers, the victims of war and abuse. All these people are a part of our world . . .

Share the words of Mary Lou Kownacki OSB as she pours out her heart for 'A Preferential Option for the Poor' (page **66**).

Let Justice Flow

Let Justice flow
into every corner of our
unjust world:
to
. . . the abused
and the accused,
the set-up
and the put-down,
the framed
and the shamed,
the battered
and the bruised,
the despairing,
and the fearing
the broken
and the bleeding,
the driven from their land
and
the bullied
and the down-trodden,
the widow
and the orphan,
the homeless
and the beggar,
the jobless
and the exploited worker,
the alone
and the lonely,
the injured
and the ill
with no pill
or potion or lotion
to soothe
and to heal . . .

... their combined clamour drowning out the sound
of lyres strumming and
pious chanting.

Susan Hardwick
England

Deir Yassin

Over the wall
a corner remains
almost inaccessible
guarded
by staring windows
dark winding tarmac

climb the wall
stumble over rubble
sun beats down
shrivelled almonds burned black
suspended from gaunt trees
brambles clutch at skirts
snake over broken tombstones
only a furtive flower
defies dereliction

soft silence of
ancient grief
hangs in the air
seeps from red soil
even the trees
spill swollen resin tears
pray
at this crumbling tomb
weep
for forgotten stories
of this place.

Patricia Price-Tomes
Israel/Palestine/England

The above poem was written following a visit to Deir Yassin, a village near Jerusalem, in sight of Yad Vashem (the Holocaust Museum). On 9 April 1948, Jewish militia carried out a massacre of Palestinian residents, as a result of which the whole population of the village fled. Over the years, Deir Yassin has come to represent the hundreds of Palestinian villages which suffered similar fates, and the continuing suffering of the Palestinian people.

The Silent People

We are the people who sometimes walk
behind your screens at newstime;
we carried our belongings
over the bridge yesterday,
today we carry our bundles
back again to our rubble.
Now the bridge is in the river.

We are the people
whose harvest failed to arrive,
whose hopes were flooded out.

We are the people with broken ploughs
and the face of hunger;
you are so used to seeing us now
you have almost ceased to notice.
Our children still have empty bellies,
and we love them
as much as you love your children.
You cannot feel our sores
and one more death is barely a statistic;
they have given up counting us now.

We are the people for whom it is nearly too late.
As you dust your ornaments
remember us

we who have burnt our carvings
to keep warm.

Cecily Taylor
England

Lord of Justice and Peace

The Church has the right and the duty to play a full part in the creation of a just society, using all the means at our disposal and in union with other believers. We pray that we, as disciples of Jesus, may know how to commit ourselves, at all levels and through concrete action, to the changing of unjust structures which imprison people in permanent oppression.

Hear us, Lord of Justice

Response: Lord of Justice and of Peace, hear our prayer.

Let us pray for rulers and heads of governments and of all international organizations, that they might strive evermore for a worldwide solidarity which assures the dignity due to people, attacking the very roots of injustice and suffering; and that they might implement effective measures to lighten the crushing debt of poorer nations.

Hear us, Lord of Justice

Response: Lord of Justice and Peace, hear our prayer.

For poor countries suffering from widespread corruption, often caused by exterior interests but exacerbated by dishonest politicians; we pray that through a renewal of conscience they might achieve harmonious and transparent management of their affairs.

Hear us, Lord of Justice

Response: Lord of Justice and Peace, hear our prayer.

We pray, too, for rich countries. May they be more aware of their duty to support the efforts of poorer neighbours to escape from poverty and misery; this is the only way to ensure the conditions necessary for a stable peace and a lasting spirit of harmony.

Hear us, Lord of Justice

Response: Lord of Justice and Peace, hear our prayer.

We pray for all those who struggle today for a just and truly human standard of life for everyone. May the Lord help them in their commitment, and may they never be discouraged by the difficulties they face.

Hear us, Lord of Justice

Response: Lord of Justice and Peace, hear our prayer.

Fr Miguel Larburu
Spain

Temple Cleansing

Sometimes the only right response is
Anger, not dull resentment,
Poisoning all it touches, or
Bitterness that taints the memory,
But a clean cutting edge, that
Lances festering grievances,
Releasing energy to fight;
The fuel of passion that
Challenges evils,

51

Outwardly observed
Or known within.

Such anger is not sin.

Ann Lewin
England

Our Global Village

Loving God, you commission us to care
for the widow and orphan,
to walk the ways of truth and mercy.
So often we fail in our global village,
where many are hungry
and some are sick and diseased.
Ours is an unequal world,
often a place of terror.
Lord, send us showers of compassion;
let streams of justice flow.
May the parched lands of oppression
become the fruitful fields of sharing.

John Johansen-Berg
England

Stranger in Our Midst

we bend twist and perjure It
to serve self-interest
foster duplicity
mask complicity
to deflect scrutiny
evade responsibility
avoid accountability
we harden our hearts
close our minds
against It

we politicize
and minimize It
we incarcerate
emasculate and
domesticate It
instead of letting It
set us free
we betray deny
and crucify It
we rarely embrace
or entertain It
It is the truth
the whole truth
and nothing but
the truth is now a stranger
in our midst

Norm S. D. Esdon
Canada

Why Them?

God, you must weep to see
The massacre of different
Innocents.
Stick limbs on swollen bellies,
Faces old before their time,
Skin stretched on grinning skulls.

We sit before the screen
And watch them die;
And from the world,
Mingling with your tears,
Comes Rachel's anguished cry
Because they are not.

And we could have helped.

Ann Lewin
England

Kapasule

I wanted to know what your village name means
but now I don't care. From today
it is clean water, a dream on paper
suddenly made real.

All those children round the gushing pump,
filling cups, bottles, drums
without the long walk home.

I sit with the village chief under the tree
beside the half-built, mud brick house
and he tells me of your plans.

Writing notes, I hear his words
and the soft beat of pigeon's wings,
but all the time the water rhythm dances in my head.
Kapasule. Kapasule. Kapasule.

Fiona Ritchie Walker
England

Golan Water

Water of life
hidden deep in wells
hoarded in tanks
drawn from lakes
distillation
of oceans.

Well, tank, lake, ocean
no matter the source
taking our taxes
they plunder our water

offer it back to us
to buy
or die.

Patricia Price-Tomes
Israel/Palestine/England

Fresh Water Is a First

If you use fair-trade sugar from Malawi or buy snacks or sweets made with it, then you have helped to make more than 500 people in Malawi very happy!

Kapasule is the first village to benefit from the fair-trade premium received by the Kasinthula Cane Growers' Association. Now local people have their own supply of clean, fresh water. Before the borehole was dug, women and children had to carry water in containers for 1.5 kms from Siseu, a nearby village. As the village chief explained, it is the first of many improvements planned for local villages, paid for with the premium.

'There are more than 500 people in the village. Only some of them are farming cane sugar, but all are benefiting from the water. They are always told that the money for this came from the sugar,' he said.

'We have plans for the future. We want to improve the local hospital and also build a community day secondary school, so that village children can get there easily.

'I want the people to be happy and the very first thing that they needed, that would make them happy, is water. Now we have one borehole. In the future, I would like us to have three.

'We would like people in the UK to buy more than they are buying now. Since the village is poor, the more people buy our sugar, the more premium we can get to help our community.'

Fiona Thomson
Traidcraft
United Kingdom

African Hand-Carved Table
(to the man who carved it)

I've no Swahili or Arabic or whatever you spoke,
so I hope English will do.

Your table seems at home in Hall Green,*
sinking its footprint into my circular rug.
Deep-cut wooden leaves and exact triangles
counterpoint the carpety-pink pseudo-Indian flowers.

You had to work hard to dig it all out
from that hefty chunk of timber,
feeling its resistance,
grunting as it yielded.
I sweat like that trying to carve out poems.

Perhaps you're with the spirits now.
The marks of your mallet and chisel
are still speaking loud:
– bold certainties,
– strange intonations,
– your basso profundo exclamations.

You flicked curly shavings from *those* grooves,
ran your finger – *there* –
and blew the dust away to see the light
in *this* sunburst
in the centre of *this* table.
You smiled at the family resemblance to your others.

Welcome, African carver,
with your twelve-sided table,
into this room where I
do my listening and praying and writing.
Join in shaping me.

Geoffrey Herbert
England

* a suburb of Birmingham UK

News from Africa
(a villanelle for the children)

I don't feel I shall ever smile again
watching that News, for now down every street
black skeletons of children haunt my brain.

They were too weak to cry, the hunger pain
that silenced them was tolling their defeat –
I don't feel I shall ever smile again.

Two slightly stronger found a farmer's grain,
he shot them as they stole one ear of wheat;
black skeletons of children haunt my brain.

The helpers fed the weakest, some in vain,
the answer was too small for all to eat.
I don't feel I shall ever smile again

this world's priorities are far too plain –
its arsenals' bellies all seven times replete.
Black skeletons of children haunt my brain

pleading for food. Our planet grows insane
to think it buys off fear, for fear's a cheat;
I don't feel I shall ever smile again –
black skeletons of children haunt my brain.

Cecily Taylor
England

Rock-crusher

Outside a town in the far south of India, some Dalit women
were squatting by the roadside breaking stone. The large grey
rocks came from the quarry. The women put up palm-leaf
shelters to provide a little shade for their babies and set to work

with hammers to break up the stone into chips that would be used for road-building. In the humid heat and over long hours, day after day, it was a hard toil.

To make life a little easier for these women the Church bought a truck and cut out the contractor bringing the rock from the quarry and delivering the chippings to the road builders so that the women could get a little more income.

But they said most of the money was taken by their husbands for drink.

So the social injustice and the human folly become the rock-crusher, grinding down the shining image of God in each person and leaving just habit, perseverance, procreation, hunger and an early death. Yet India can afford to build nuclear weapons. And that is our world, brilliant and deadly, splendid and miserable.

> Dalit women, teach us;
> waken our conscience;
> destroy our self-satisfaction;
> call us to share the good things of life,
> and keep on calling
> so that even Washington and Downing Street
> and Kremlin and World Bank may hear you.

> *Bernard Thorogood*
> *Australia*

Christmas Card

> The figures are the same:
> The tender curves of
> A mother cradling her child.
> But there is no breastful of milk
> To satisfy this infant
> Whose cries of hunger echo her own.
> Their eyes look blankly
> At a world which offers little hope.

Come on, ye faithful,
And all people of goodwill,
It is time to be midwives
For the love of God
Struggling again to birth;
Deliver healing
To our crying world.

Ann Lewin
England

Let the World Be Changed
(Just Share)

Chorus:
Let the world be changed
Let the rules be changed
Let there be a place foreveryone
Bring God's Kingdom near
Let all be welcome here
and may there be for all a just share

The scales of world trade are unbalanced and unfair
Between the rich world and the poor
we let faith restore hope that the rules can be changed
So bringing a just share to all

Chorus:
Let the world be changed . . .

Let's break bread together in a broken world
Let's share the bread and together make a vow
That the poor of the world wherever they may be
May come and join the world's table now.

Chorus:
Let the world be changed . . .

There are tariffs that keep the rich world rich
And patents that keep the poor world out
If we sow injustice we'll reap calamity
It's time to change the trade rules now.

Chorus :
Let the world be changed . . .

Garth Hewitt
England

Acts of God

A Reflection on Rights
Based on material from Acts 6–8, 9, 16, 18 and 22–27; Romans 6.1

The fact that Stephen's death led to evangelism and church
 growth
– doesn't make stoning people right.

The fact that God found Paul on the way to Damascus
– doesn't make persecution right.

The fact that a Philippian jailer was led to faith by two of his
 prisoners
– doesn't make it right to imprison people without proper
 trial.

The fact that Priscilla and Aquila did good church work in
 Corinth and Ephesus
– doesn't make it right that the emperor threw Jews out of
 Rome.

The fact that Paul's shipwreck brought the gospel to Malta
– doesn't make it right that he had to travel to get justice.

The fact that grace abounds
– doesn't make it right when our world continues in sin

If God can work in a world full of wrongs
– what might God do in a world that cared about rights?

John Proctor
England

AIDS

Weaw*
She lies dying!
AIDS has taken over,
Wasting a young innocent life.
Mercy!

But why?
Just twelve years old!
No more tears from her eyes.
What has she done to deserve death?
Tell me!

Children
Dying of AIDS,
Suffering and hopeless,
So alone, often unwanted.
God, why?

Salvador T. Martinez
Thailand

* Weaw was a Thai girl who was born with HIV and died of HIV/AIDS
complex at twelve years old.

In God's Agenda

(written for people with AIDS who feel they have no future)

I have many tears and sorrows.
There has been a time
When I didn't know what's right or wrong.
I kept the right one out
And the wrong one in.
Nobody knows the trouble I see –
Who'll set me free from bondage?
I have many questions for tomorrow.
So scared about my future
Into the darkness I will go.
Darkness will imprison me
Tears from my eyes will flow like a river
Because my days are uncertain.

> *Be still and know that I am God*
> *Lay your burden on my shoulder.*

Hallelujah, it's the words of the living God.
He who came to love, heal and forgive
Will heal my future
I'm in his agenda
In justice he will solve my problems.
My days may be uncertain
Yet I can face it because he will make it for me.

Samuel Pachuau
North-East India

'Standing Near the Cross . . .'
(John 19.25)

My younger son received an HIV positive diagnosis six years ago. I am thankful for the excellent treatment and support available to him through our National Health Service in the

UK and to voluntary organisations which offer support, but I feel the pain of the injustice which so many people with HIV/AIDS have to bear, on top of their illness, in all those places where they are unable to get the treatment and support they so desperately need. This prayer is for them.

Mary, Mother of God,
stand beside all mothers
who watch the suffering
of innocent children
in every place of crucifixion today;

in places of poverty, anguish and despair,
where medication is rationed or denied
because someone else holds the purse strings,
and dictates spending priorities;

in places of fragile hope,
and committed action,
where grandmothers,
aunties and surrogate mothers
combine their efforts
to bring light and love
to children, orphaned by AIDS,
or infected from birth;

in places of fragile hope
and self-giving love,
where older brothers and sisters
became carers too soon,
parenting and providing for their families
when fathers and mothers have died.

Mary, Mother of God,
give strength to all
who feel powerless
in the face of such pain;

lift up their hearts
to sing 'Magnificat';
to cry 'Freedom'
for all whose lives have
been brought low;
to raise the voice
of prophecy and protest
in the corridors of power;
to proclaim the love
and justice of God
for all who are
marginalised or oppressed.

Mary, Mother of God,
may they rest in your compassion
and take your courage
into their hands.

Jean Mortimer
England

Power Games

When we play God
We throw our weight around,
Treat people like chess pieces,
Play our games regardless of their
Gifts. Their value lies in
Cost-effectiveness, not in
Intrinsic worth. And if we lose,
We simply change the rules
And use them to our own advantage.

Lord, it must sometimes
Break your heart, to see how
We mismanage your creation,
Misuse freedom. Are you sometimes
Tempted to break our teeth,

Hurl thunderbolts, cry
Halt?

It must be most
Frustrating
Being
God.

Ann Lewin
England

Bed and Breakfast

I live sheltered by the name
For a cheap holiday.
Some holiday. A family of slugs
Lives in the bathroom, mice scurry
Grey as fear. There is the occasional
Rat. But what I mind most is being
Squashed with the children in one room,
Loving, fighting, eating, sleeping
Publicly; queueing to use facilities
Stained by others' existence.
So, I have a roof. Must I always be
Thankful for small mercies?
What I want is a home.
Sod your trickle down economy,
The only thing that trickles here is
Rain, relentlessly through the ceiling.
Trickle, God, can't you send a flood,
Justice in torrents to carry me to my
Dream home? Nothing elaborate: just
Damp-free, no fungus in the corners;
The only creatures there present by
Invitation; water running through pipes;
Space, privacy. Not much to ask.

Ann Lewin
England

Prayer for Charity
and
A Preferential Option for the Poor

Poor Ones,
Please take the bread. It is yours.
The house with running water belongs to you.
A plot of land, a dignified job – all yours.
Forgive me for offering it.
Charity is no substitute for justice
but your children are hungry now.

Spirit of Justice, break open our hearts.
Break them wide open.

Let anger pour through like strong winds
cleaning us of complacency.

Let courage pour through like spring storms
flooding out fear.

Let zeal pour through like blazing summer sun,
Filling us with passion.

Force of Justice, grant me anger,
courage to do what must be done,
passion to break down the walls of injustice
and build a land flowing with milk and honey
for God's beloved,
God's special love,
God's Poor Ones.

Spirit of Justice
Break open our hearts.

Mary Lou Kownacki OSB
USA

A Prayer for Human Rights Day

Leader: God of all,
You know the vulnerable beauty of human life

Response: **Through Jesus Christ you live among us**

Leader: You know the mystery of human love

Response: **Through Jesus Christ you transform our relationships**

Leader: You know the depths of human fear and cruelty

Response: **Through Jesus Christ you bear our sins**

Leader: You know the agony of human terror and pain

Response: **Through Jesus Christ you cry with us**

Leader: We hold before you, O God, those sisters and
brothers in Asia,
Tortured, humiliated, despised,
In body, mind or spirit,
Their human dignity harshly denied
Their human rights brutally violated

We particularly remember before you women and men who are undergoing human rights violations in (name the countries in current news) and other suffering people and troubled places close to our hearts.

Silence

Leader: We pray for people in these countries who have
been denied human dignity and human rights
based on race, class, sex, nationality, ideology
and faith.

Their rights are being denied every day through misuse of power at national and international levels;

through authoritarian, repressive, military regimes;

through anti-people policies and

through the abuse of technology which endangers the earth and all life upon it.

Silence

Leader: Embrace all these victims with your courage and compassion.

Convert the hard hearts of the cruel with your love.

Bring justice to your people in a stream of healing and renewal.

Show us afresh, the precious gift of being human.

Give us the grace and wisdom to act faithfully according to your divine love.

Strengthen our faith that life in you is stronger than death can ever be.

We pray in your name, Jesus Christ our Lord **Amen.**

*Christian Conference of Asia
Hong Kong*

The Trouble with An Asylum Seeker
(A reflection on experience, with the help of Laban and Jethro)

'Esau is planning to kill you. Flee at once.' Jacob left. And Laban brought him to his house.
(Genesis 27.42–43; 28.10; 29.13)

Pharaoh sought to kill Moses. But Moses fled from Pharaoh. The priest of Midian invited him to stay with him.
(Exodus 2.15–21)

The trouble with an asylum
seeker is
that he might fancy your
daughter.

So you could make him work
for you,
and cheat and deceive him,
and put a hefty price-tag on
their love,
and keep a close eye on all
they do.

You might be so edgy with
him,
that the corners of his
character
became as sharp as yours

And all he would want would
be
to get free again,
to run away once more,
from your caution and control

You would end up losing your
daughter,
in devious disputes
over animals and lesser gods.

And the story of salvation,
would leave you behind
as a marginal note
in a corner

The thing about an asylum
seeker is
that he might fancy your
daughter.

If you were prepared to see
love grow,
you might find you could
trust him
with your own concerns and
wealth,
even when he was out of
your sight.

You might trust him so
much,
that he found the confidence
to hear the voice of God.

And God might call him
away,
to lead a people to freedom,
in answer to the summons,
you helped him to hear.

you would feel you had
found a son,
when you helped him bring
justice
to God's holy people.

And the story of salvation,
would go forward
with you as a link
in the chain.

69

as a man who took,
when he could have given so
   much
and might have prevented
the birth of a nation.

as a man who gave himself,
to a nation not his own,
and helped them become
the people God intended.

The trouble with an asylum
   seeker,
is that when you take him in,
you start seeing
more of what you're really
   like.

The thing about an asylum
   seeker,
is that when you take him in,
you might discover
more about the goodness of
   God.

(Based on Genesis 27–31)

(Based on Exodus 2, 3 and 18)

John Proctor
England

Move Towards Justice for All People
(inspired by Becoming the Church of the Stranger –
Christian Conference of Asia)

Leader: Prompt and prod us Lord to grow churches in
our communities

People: **that will be courageous and challenge those
who live by 'comfort the afflicted' to 'afflict the
comfortable'.**

Leader: Prompt and prod us Lord to grow churches in
our communities

People: **that will not only talk about peace but demand
justice and work toward an active peace.**

Leader: Prompt and prod us Lord to grow churches in
our communities

People:	that will not remain silent when persecuted people are pleading for their voices to be heard; that will not pass by on the other side; that will walk in solidarity with despairing, terrified women and men.
Leader:	Prompt and prod us Lord to grow churches in our communities
People:	that will witness to the fact that Christ calls us to love our neighbour – with no strings attached – and to follow Christ even when the way points to a cross.
All:	We offer ourselves to walk the way of Jesus Christ and to serve all humanity especially the people who are suffering, wherever those friends may be situated, because of the greed and the hypocrisy of those in power.

Geoffrey Duncan
England

You'll Find Me
(Oscar Romero, Archbishop of San Salvador)

You know where to find me
and what I am, conservative by nature,
not young, no wild one; yet
God's vicar, here: protector of the weak;

constrained to do my duty
by your repression of the poor, the very
excesses of your deeds;
the thousands that cry of brutality

from where you've consigned them.
You see no value in them, but our God
believes in them so much
he identifies himself with each of them.

Can a mere man, be he
clerk, peasant or archbishop, do less, if
he says he follows Christ?
He, you, set my agenda, not myself.

Here I am, daily in
my pulpit, kneeling at the altar in
the house of God. You know
just where to find me, and I know you'll come.

I'm not afraid of death
for if I die I'll live. You'll find me in
The people of San Salvador.
But now, what breath you leave for me

I give to those who look
to me, and give them, in God's name, my words,
His love: 'I, you: God's poor,
today, elect of heaven, we are one.'

Brian Louis Pearce
England

Malawi Prayers
Based on interviews with women sugar cane farmers at Kasinthula, Malawi.

For two parts:
Leader and Sugar Farmer (Farmer part can be one voice or
several people).

Leader
Lord we pray for the sugar farmers in Malawi and for all people
who grow and harvest the foods that we enjoy.

Farmer

Every morning at four o'clock, Monday to Friday, I am going into the garden and starting hard work. To survive, it is difficult.

Leader

Bless those who are working in the sugar cane fields.

Farmer

We work hard in the fields. We are working there for six or seven hours, then we go home and start work doing the daily chores.

Leader

Bless their families and the communities in which they live.

Farmer

The sugar cane has helped me a lot. I am the only member of my house that is earning money. I use it to buy food for my family.

Leader

Lord, we thank you that through fair trade, families are being fed.

Farmer

Now we have fresh water in my village.

Leader

We thank you, Lord, for fresh water and the living water that you give us through Jesus.

Farmer

My hopes for my grandchildren are mostly education.

Leader

We thank you that children are receiving a better education and a better future.

Farmer

When people in the UK buy our sugar, you are helping us to improve our livelihoods.

Leader

Lord, we thank you that our actions here can change the lives of people on the other side of the world. We pray that as Christians we may lead the way in putting faith into action, bringing justice to your people. Amen.

Fiona Thomson
Traidcraft
United Kingdom

Sealed in Concrete

In April 2000, in a scene reminiscent of biblical times, a Bedouin shepherd boy was playing a haunting tune on his pipe as he watched his goats on a hillside east of Bethlehem. An eagle soared overhead. In the fertile valley below, close to an ancient threshing floor, was a cistern, which had fed the valley with water for many hundreds of years. Ancient channels dug in the surrounding hillsides led the rainwater to the cistern, and from there to the valley floor. But like so many cisterns we had encountered on our hundred-mile walk from the northernmost reaches of Palestine, along the eastern hills of the West Bank, this one was sealed with concrete. 'Oh no,' groaned Mark, the Palestinian organiser of the walk: 'this cistern was open when I passed it two weeks ago.' Kefar, one of our fellow walkers, a Moslem from Ramallah, sat down, his head in his hands. A sombre, depressed silence descended upon us. As we approached Bethlehem, another shepherd lamented that soon, without access to water, he would be forced to move elsewhere. The valley would become parched enabling the Israelis to plant another settlement on supposedly 'unused' land. The beauty of the valley, rich in biblical history, nurtured by generations of Palestinians, belied the tragedy which was facing it, and which faced so many of the valleys through which we had walked in the West Bank, where ancient cisterns have been

sealed and even blown up to force out the indigenous people
from their land.

Andrew Ashdown
England

The People of the West
(Amos Rides Again)

You've silenced your prophets
You've shot down your dreamers
Your life-blood is money
You're exploiting the poor

Oh the people of the West just love to invest
In the system that keeps the poor man poor

You have no compassion
Your lifestyle is evil
Higher living standard
The God you adore

Oh the people of the West just love to invest
In the system that keeps the poor man poor

Chorus:
But let justice roll on like a river
And truth like an ever-flowing stream
Then tears of rage will turn to laughter
And people become what they should be

You ignore the ways of justice
Though you talk a lot about it
You victimise the stranger
Seeking refuge in your land

Oh the people of the West just love to invest
In the system that keeps the poor man poor

Greed is your mother
Silence is your father
Your epitaph is written
In frustrated tears of rage

Oh the people of the West just love to invest
In the system that keeps the poor man poor

Chorus:
But let justice . . .

Garth Hewitt
England

Inside Out

Black, white and gold
Are the colours of life –

For sorrow is black;
And the small seed of kindness
Unseen;
And the velvet of night
That hides love . . .

And the colour of skin.

For whiteness is pure,
And the breathless potential
Of dawn
Is revealed in the light
That hides nothing . . .

And the colour of skin.

For gold is of joy;
And the shining of sunlight
Unspent;

And the heat of the fire
That heals all . . .

And the colour of skin.

If the colours of life
Are the colours of skin –
Which clothes and encloses
The essence within –

Then the blood and the tears
Are the same.

Margot Arthurton
England

Poppy Is Her Name

Fallow may be the field
but from the soil at rest
a host of flowers springs,
a mass of scarlet poppies rose
on slender hairy stems
and turn crushed silken petals
translucent to the sun.

Why do I gasp in wonder at the sight
of scarlet splotches random on the green
yet turn away in pity and revulsion
from random blotches
on a young girl's skin?

She walked into the hall
and people looked – and looked away.
Her fair young skin was spotted
dark and brown unevenly.
Her eyes were clear and grey

and nothing in her manner showed
how leprous she appeared.

Now, standing in the field of poppies
suddenly I saw her – beautiful –
like scarlet poppies on a sea of green,
and like the morning sun God's love
was shining through.

I do not know her name
but in my mind
I'll think of her as 'Poppy'.

Helene McLeod
England

Love Kindness

Our tithes are worthless without love,
for all that God desires
is justice for the fatherless,
the end of terror's fires.

O let us listen, till we hear
the cry of the oppressed
who call for mercy, then respond,
that fears may be addressed.

Love kindness, humbly walk with God
and, through compassion, trace
the person we are called to love
in each and every face.

Andrew Pratt
England

The Humble Cup of Tea

Leader   The earth is the Lord's and all things in it.

Reader 1   Mountains and mornings, evenings and animals, forests and food, all part of God's limitless creativity.

Reader 2   Even the humble cup of tea . . .

Reader 1   . . . is more complex that we might think.

Leader   More than 3,000 varieties of tea, all from the leaves of one plant –

Reader 2   – *Camellia sinensis.*

Leader   Evergreen . . . and really a tree . . . without pruning, growing to twelve or fourteen metres.

Reader 1   Properly looked after, it can last for over eighty years.

Leader   In a well-managed plantation, under good conditions . . .

Reader 2   . . . harvesting takes place every seven to ten days.

Reader 1   All done by hand because leaves must be carefully selected.

Leader   So many people working . . . Plantations with whole families relying on work for wages, food, homes, healthcare . . .

Reader 2   . . . and education.

Leader	A way of earning a living for small-scale farmers too.
Reader 1	And every leaf plucked must be processed on the day it is picked.
Leader	So many people ...
Reader 2	Such a short time ...
Reader 1	So few companies dominating the tea industry ...
Reader 1	Millions of people ...
Reader 2	Millions of cups of tea ...
Leader	In the UK we drink more tea than the rest of Europe put together.[1]
Reader 1	Our favourite drink ...
Reader 2	144 million cups drunk every day[2] ...
Reader 1	... most of them not fairly traded ...
Leader	... which means millions of people not thinking about others
Reader 2	... not asking what their money is buying
Leader	... not looking for the Fairtrade Mark, not helping others to earn a decent wage, to have good working conditions.
Reader 1	Such a simple step, helping others by thinking about what we buy.

[1] EFTA Yearbook 2001–3
[2] BBC1 website

Reader 2	Simple as switching on the kettle, pouring out a refreshing cup of tea at the end of a busy day. Relaxing, knowing you've earned it.
Leader	Who'd like a nice cup of tea?

Fiona Thomson
Traidcraft
United Kingdom

Prayer for the Tea Chain

Lord the next time I drink a cup of tea
help me to remember
those who
prepared the land,
nurtured the tea bushes,
picked and processed the leaves,
bought and sold them –
all those who helped to bring this drink to my table.

Lord the next time I buy tea
help me to remember
my part in the tea chain,
the way that when I choose fair trade
I can help producers to get a better deal
and work their way out of poverty.

Lord the next time I am served a cup of tea
help me to spread the good news of fair trade
and encourage more people to add it to their shopping list.

Fiona Thomson
Traidcraft
United Kingdom

Suffer Little Children . . .

Remember the inner-city-child,
caught up in a web of violence
and abuse
and crime.
The threads woven so fine
that entrapment
is a foregone conclusion.

Remember the street-child,
begging on the street
vulnerable to all
the evil that stalks it.

Remember the orphan-child,
so alone and lonely
in a frightening
and uncaring world.

Remember the hungry-child,
belly swollen
with lack of food
silently sobbing because
there is no strength left for sound.

Remember the exploited-child,
despairingly or past-caringly
selling their bodies
for the perverted desires
of evil men.

Remember the Christ-child,
Who came to create
a new world order
by showing us how
we should love and care.

So
If we have learned *anything* at all
why are there still so *many*
suffering children?

Susan Hardwick
                                          England

Ragged Child

Whose is the child,
The ragged child,
Who runs wild
On the tip,
And fights for the crumbs
Discarded –
Thrown by those who have
Too much
To such
As he?

What sort of living,
Scavenging,
Raging for scraps
Thrown in scorn
Does he make?
Desperation sees him take
From smaller, thinner hands;
For need sees nothing
But its own
Starving belly,
And eats compassion
For the lack of better nourishment.

So do we shut our eyes to this
Catastrophe?
Does it disappear behind
Our darkening lids?

Do we ignore the brazen sky
That starves the world we cannot see,
And brings no rain or growing?
Are we doing this

And knowing?

Whose is the child,
The ragged child?

He is ours.

Margot Arthurton
England

There Is Much I Would Do

There is much I would do for you, my friend;
but, you see, you are not of my skin.
There is much I could say that would ease your way
and, although I am blessed with means and ends,
I must save what I can for my kin.

There is hope I would give if I could, my friend;
but, you speak a tongue strange to my ear
and, although God above has called me to love,
I apologise for my hesitant trend
and must love only those I hold dear.

I would help you if I had time, my friend;
but you cannot expect me to alter.
I have worked hard to grab the chances I've had.
And, although you say you need help to mend,
It's not my fault your fortune has faltered.

Of course I will bless you today, my friend,
even though you are not of my race.
I can wish you good speed and direct you to feed

at the soup kitchen just round the bend.
Yes, I am brimming with Christian grace.

Duncan L. Tuck
England

A Malaysian Woman
(who lives her life in a wheelchair)

To be disabled,
to be a woman
and to be a dark-skinned Indian
is to be trebly disadvantaged
and discriminated against
in our Malaysian society;
so where is justice?

A Malaysian Woman

I'm not just a Back

I'm not just a back
I'm complete
I have a front, sides
a top
and a bottom.

I do the things you do
but slower
and with pain.
Take stock and look around
while waiting for me to catch up.

I have a voice
and my essence, my being
can run like the wind
I can go forward as well as backwards.

*Jayne Greathead
England*

85

The Prayers of the People

The symbols are brought forward during the prayers or they may be placed on a table covered with a cloth and brought forward at the preparation of Gifts if there is a celebration of the Eucharist. Or they may remain on the table throughout the worship.

Let us pray:

Silence

> We remember before God all those who have been uprooted
> from their homes and communities;
> people who are compelled to flee for their lives,
> to leave their land and culture,
> and live apart from their families.

> With them, we mourn their loss of dignity, community,
> resources and employment.

A globe, map or small bag with a few items of clothing may be brought forward as symbols of those who are uprooted.

> We especially pray for the women
> who are the majority of those displaced.

> We remember the work that women do
> to keep families together,
> to nurture community
> and end violence and injustice.

A shawl or scarf may be brought forward.

> We remember the millions of children
> whose lives are marked by danger and exploitation.

A child's worn shoe or a small toy may be brought forward.

We remember those who are persecuted
     because of their gender, race or creed.

We pray for the women and men,
     the children and the elderly,
     who seek safety and solace,
     who yearn to begin new lives.

For all the uprooted,

**Sheltering God, in your mercy,
Hear our prayer.**

We remember before God
     those countries where people must leave their homes
     because of war, injustice and violence.

*A figure of a dove, a paper crane or a flower may be brought forward
as symbols of peace.*

We remember those places
     which have been made unsafe by landmines,
     and all those who have been killed or maimed by
          landmines.

We remember those in our own homeland
     who live with violence and its brutal threat.

For all people terrified by violence.

**Gentle God, in your mercy
Hear our prayer.**

We pray for those who leave their homes for economic
     survival;
     we remember that the gap between rich and poor gets
          wider,
     and the earth's resources are shared by fewer people.

Pennies, newspaper clippings or items relevant to the country/ community in which this prayer is prayed may be brought forward as symbols of economic survival.

We pray for those who pay the cost of international debt
    with their lives.

We remember the homeless and poorly housed
    and the unemployed in our own communities.

For all people displaced by economic disparity,

**God of Justice, in your mercy,
Hear our prayer.**

We remember before God
    those who leave their homes because of earthquakes,
    storms, floods and other disasters.

We acknowledge the effects of deforestation,
    degradation of farm land,
    nuclear and weapons testing,
    and the exploitation of resources
    for the sake of consumers in other countries.

A pot of earth or an uprooted plant may be brought forward as symbols of the environment.

We remember those in our own communities
    who have been hurt by poor stewardship of creation.

For all people displaced by devastation of your world.

**Creator God, in your mercy,
Hear our prayer.**

We give thanks to you, God,
for the world's diversity of people and cultures.

A multi-coloured braid of wool, kaleidoscope or rainbow may be brought forward as symbols of diversity.

We pray that hostility and indifference
may give way to hospitality and justice
in *(name your own country)* and throughout the world

Help us to be vigilant stewards and faithful partners,
and strengthen us to live as people of your creation,
committed and bold in deeds of justice.

God of all,
you taught us through your Son
to seek the signs of your reign
in the tiny mustard seed.
Plant your word in the soil of our hearts,
sow in us the seeds of compassion;
let your hospitality take root within us,
and your compassion grow in us,
so righteousness may spring forth in all the world,
and your holy will be done.
We ask this in his name.
Amen.

Members of the congregation are invited to come forward and plant a seed as a sign of hope and to name the hope aloud concluding with the words 'Come Holy Spirit'.

Response

**Renew the face of the earth
and the hearts of your people.**

The Peace

The peace of the Lord always be with you.

And also with you.

Primate's World Relief and Development Fund
Anglican Church of Canada

God of Mercy and of Grace

God of mercy and of grace,
you constantly startle and surprise us;
you shake us out of casual complacency;
you reveal your presence to us
in unexpected places
at unexpected times
through unexpected people
and in unexpected forms.
As we reflect on the reality of violence in our societies,
as we ponder the violence experienced by your Son,
enable us to be receptive and responsive,
awake and alert to the demands of the gospel,
rededicating ourselves to live out our faith in action
working towards the restoration of wholeness
and the possibility of healing.
This we pray in and through the present and
    coming One, Jesus,
whose death resulted in breaking down the dividing walls
    of hostility.
Amen

J. Jayakiran Sebastian
South India

Not Alone

Wilberforce, the
Venns
and Thornton did
their best work when

met with others
as
the Clapham Sect:
gathered *en masse*
at prayer, bent on
see-
ing slavery
abolished. We

can still feel them:
im-
pelled by faith through
Gospel and hymn,

and of immense
de-
cision and
capacity.

A nurse who came
from
her Guyana
and saw the tomb

of Wilberforce
in
the *Abbey*,* awed,
drew her breathe in.

* *Westminster Abbey, London UK*

Generations
later,
at the name of
her, Liberator'.

Brian Louis Pearce
England

Holy Spirit, Breathe Your Comfort

Holy Spirit,
you who always breathes new life
into your world,
come with healing wind
to us in this moment.
Breathe your comfort to all who despair,
breathe your healing to all who are wounded,
breathe your presence to all who feel abandoned,
breathe your courage to all who are frightened,
breathe your warmth to all who are freezing,
breathe your spring time to all sceptical ones,
breathe your love to all who have been hurt
     in the name of love,
breathe your future to all who have given up.

Per Harling
Sweden

My Mother in Heaven

Mother in Heaven,
paternity can only limit your grace.
To call you Mother God
shortens the distance between humanity and divinity.

I don't need a military Father God.
After studying about warfare,
I'm fed up with masculinity
the result is only violence!

92

Can we have a more civilised way
to sort out our conflicts?
Why do we have to use a gun,
to shoot and kill?

As a Mother,
you know how to care and treasure life.
You understand our feelings more truly
have sympathy on our emotion more deeply.
How can a father-image compare with your masculinity?

You create life
You are the Mother of Eve
The Mother of our mothers.
You know the price for just one single human.
You cry if just a single one is lost and killed.

As I'm in despair
your comfort will stand by me
my sorrow and suffering
is your grief and agony.

Wong Mei Yuk
Hong Kong

Witnesses

What a rich heritage is theirs
and what a long line of witnesses they form.
These are the women of courage
who stand out in every generation.
Mary Magdalene, Mary, mother of James,
Joanna and Salome,
who came to the tomb of Jesus
early on the resurrection day.
The martyrs of the early church,
Pelagia, Perpetua and Felicity,

who gave their lives
rather than deny their faith.
The women of the Black Sash,
who made a courageous witness against apartheid.
The mothers for peace in Russia
who were not cowed by a communist state.
The women of Greenham Common*
who endured wind, rain and cold frost
to make a stand against nuclear bombs.

There have been many in every generation,
and in many places and situations,
women who have opposed injustice,
stood alongside the oppressed
and witnessed for freedom at great cost.
Their names are written
in the Lamb's Book of life.

John Johansen-Berg
England

* Greenham Common, UK where women had a
  permanent camp to oppose nuclear weapons.

I Am Wonderfully Made

What is so wrong with me and my being
That they say I am not as good as a man?
That I cannot be equal to a man?
And therefore I cannot be treated fairly like a man?

Is it because of my body, with its cycles and changes?
But God created me a woman –
flesh and blood, organs and cells, skin and bones
my body may not be the same as a man's but still
I, too, am wonderfully made.

Is it because my brawn is different from that of a man?
But God created me a woman –
my muscles and bones may not have been honed like a man's

but give me time to catch up, to learn, and to practise
for I am just as wonderfully made.

Is it because my brain does not think and analyse
the same things as much as a man?
But God created me a woman –
I feel as I think and I do think many things,
all the time and often at the same time –
Family, school, budget, children, food, home,
the present and the future and the list never ends . . .
And so, I know that I am wonderfully made.

O Loving Mystery,
How could I be a mistake, an accident, an after-thought
that you would have created me inferior or secondary to a
    man?
How could you will me to be lower than a man because of
    my blood flow –
When that is the same life-giving source that creates and
    nurtures life itself?
How could my body and being be violated with insults,
    abuse and neglect
when I am also created in your own image?

Dear Loving Mystery,
please give me the will to appreciate my body
give me the strength to affirm my sexuality.
You made me the way I am
and I am wonderfully made.

Hope S. Antone
Malaysia

Woman You Are Called . . .

You are woman

You are woman –
    Strong soaring with wings far stretched into the horizon
    Reaching to the heights

Bowing to the depths.

You are woman –
Strong – reaching out to other women and together –
Discovering the depths of relationships
With self
With family
With community
With creation

You are woman –
Strong – learning and re-learning
Shouting from the depths of your being
        the integrity of these relationships
The profound insight that's
        grounded in solid granite

Food embargo

Red lips,
White lips!

            Bright eyes,
            Dull eyes!

                        Rosy cheeks,
                        Pale cheeks!

Policies and decisions drawn in the board rooms,
        carpeted floors and air-conditioned rooms.
Along the street sits a woman tired and weak
Around her neck tiny arms embraced
        tiny hands outstretched
'A bowl of thin rice gruel, please, madam, sir!'
The voice trails on
The figures to invisibility.

Red lips,
White lips!

Bright eyes,
Dull eyes!

Rosy cheeks,
Pale cheeks!

Tell me what is fair.
Tell me what is just.
Help me understand.

Sr Bibiana Bunuan
Phillipines/Tanzania/USA

3

A Rainbow World

I was a stranger and you welcomed me.
Matthew 25.35

Reconciliation is one of the key factors of the Gospels. Accept all of humankind whoever and wherever they are, especially the people who have lost their families through war and violence, the people who have been turned out of their villages, those people who have lost their homes – the refugees who suffer increasingly as a result of ruthless people, the asylum seekers who flee for their lives after terrifying experiences, degradation, rape, torture and related atrocities.

Open Our Hearts
Open Our Minds
Open Our Hands

Patricia Price-Tomes, who has spent time in Palestine reminds us of a 'Twenty-first-century nativity – Palestinian style', (page **119**).
Let us look to 'The River of Hope – A Children's Liturgy' as portrayed by the National Council of Churches, Australia on (page **109**).

Rainbow World

Red, Orange, Yellow and Green,
Indigo, Violet and Blue –
all together reflecting
your great love
of diversity.

Not just White and Black
for your great vision.
Rather,
you shade in your world
with all the colours
of the rainbow.

I can picture you now,
at the dawn
of creation:
your artist's brush and palette
and painting in every
shade and hue.

Creator God,
fill us with that same sense
of excitement
and wonder
and delight
as you,
at such richness
of diversity.

Susan Hardwick
England

Lord, No One Is a Stranger to You

Lord, no one is a stranger to you
and no one is ever far from
your loving care.
In your kindness watch over refugees
and exiles,
those separated from their loved one,
young people who are lost,
and those who have left or run away
from home.
Bring them back safely to the place
where they long to be
and help us always to show your kindness
to strangers and to those in need.

CAFOD
England

The Pattern of Strangers

Lord, break us and bless our breaking up,
That each meeting with strangers may crack our
   expectations
Every glance born in another continent chip away our
   narrow complacency.

Lord, melt us and hallow our uncertainties,
That the approach of different cultures may cause second
   thoughts about our own,
The intermingling of traditions throw a critical eye on our
   values.

Lord, shake us and honour our unsteady footing,
That the surety of other faiths may make us seek the rock
   we rest on,

The rich diversity we encounter prompt us, more carefully,
   to choose our path.

Lord, mould us from the clays of our experience,
That within the people you are forming we allow each
   stranger, each experience,
To leave a thumb mark, and so enhance your pattern for our
   lives.

Duncan L. Tuck
England

Refugees (1)

They stream across our screens
Balancing impossible burdens;
The remnants of their lives
Tied up in bundles.
Yet what we see is nothing
To the burdens they carry
In their hearts:
Loss, pain and fear.

Ann Lewin
England

Portable Things

When we are given the signs,
Old signs, which are always the same,
We drag from our wardrobes tough boots,
Kiss goodbye, forever, door-frames.
We lock, forever, full houses.
Set our feet on the road again.

We take only portable things;
Small ones, to keep us from cold.

Things of high value and priceless
Which always we've carried.

There's gold
Sewn into seams on our coats.
And the diamonds which adorned our ladies
We'll sell in the promised lands.

And, bound in our arms, babies.

Lucy Berry
                                                    England

The Orchard

I am a woman who lives in a large and fruitful orchard, a veritable paradise. I was born here. In my early years I thrived on the fruit offered to me by my parents and shared with those living in the same part of the orchard. As I grew up I was able to explore more of the orchard, so I learnt to share its fruits with others I met; swapping, giving and receiving a wide range of fruits throughout my life.

As I reflect on it now, the main part of my diet is probably made up of a relatively small range of fruits. At one time it was smaller than it is now. This mix has and still does constantly change. There have always been some fruits I have preferred to others such that I have actively looked for them, or waited impatiently for them to come into season for another year. Over time I've tasted more different fruits and some I've eagerly added to my regular diet. Others I'm more ambivalent about and there are some I wouldn't care to taste again in a hurry

From time to time someone will come with a spoilt fruit saying 'What shall we do with this?' or perhaps just silent, head bowed, eyes red. Then it's a job to know what to do. Mostly I, like the majority here, go on swapping, giving and receiving the fruits, ever mindful of just how marvellous this orchard is.

From time to time a new discovery is made somewhere in the orchard and there's a celebration

The orchard is usually very fruitful. Some people just ignore the bad fruits, pretend they're not there, treading them into the grass they pick something else. Others are more sensitive. When there's a glut of something and heaps go to waste, some get quite angry. Equally in lean times there are some people who will always share their last fruit with you. I think I could safely say I've had my moments when I've been each of these.

I've had different roles in the orchard but I still prefer the vital business of swapping, giving and receiving fruit. It's life giving.

Of course there are moments when the orchard is the last place I want to be; when arguments break out over fruit or lack of them, or a whinge goes round about 'how the orchard has changed' or 'we don't do it like that' or 'it'll never work'. And of course it can be really tiring just dealing with all this fruit.

When that happens there are a number of things I do. I might make my way to the edge of the orchard and look out beyond at the contrasts in the landscape and wonder what it is like there. Or I might climb to the top of a tree and look across the swaying sea of branches. Or I might nestle down in the grass to plant a pip or stone, or to admire a tiny seedling already sprouting, where one was planted previously.

It's at these times that I commit myself again to the swapping, giving and receiving of fruit that goes on in the orchard and get ready, with an open mind, to swap another fruit with my neighbour.

Janet Lees
England

Lord, Clear Our Eyes

Lord, clear our eyes that we may see the suffering of the
   refugee.
Open our ears that we may hear the cries of those in deep
   despair.
Release our feet that we may walk on paths where some
   comfort we may spread.
Unloose our tongues that we might speak your words of
   hope and love.
Give us open hearts that we may truly welcome the stranger
   in our midst.

National Council of Churches
Australia

Asylum Seekers

They live under the shadow of
A two-edged sword: in a place of safety
And a state of fear. The rules
Ensure we are kept safe; our fear
Defines our hospitality,
Keeps them on edge.
Compassion is constrained
By a prudent care.

Could we, instead of seeing problems.
Begin to recognise the gifts they bring,
And be enriched by their humanity?

Ann Lewin
England

Marianne

Marianne goes every week
To visit the Art Therapist.
She saw some things in Kosovo
Which gave her youthful mind a twist.

And she won't sleep without a light
And she eats hour by hour by hour.
She follows daddy everywhere
And stamps on every ant and flower.

She leaves school early once a week
To go and have her therapy.
Her mother, anxious and afraid,
Comes on those days to talk with me.

'She draws her father, draws the sky.
She draws some guns. She draws her bed.
She draws her sister and a knife.
And everything she draws is red.'

Lucy Berry
England

My Friend

Could I call you friend, whose face I cannot see,
    shrouded as you are from male gaze?
Shall I call you friend, whose name I do not know,
    anonymous within the urban maze?
Would I were your friend, to know you in your home
    and see your clan and your domestic ways.
And if you were my friend, you'd share with me your heart
    to clear the fog of ignorance, this haze.
So here's my open hand, my open face, my hope
    for friendship that will beautify our days.

Bernard Thorogood
Australia

Refugees (2)

Lord, we ask your pardon for our ignorance
of the plight of the refugees in our country.
Lord have mercy   *Lord have mercy*

Lord, we ask pardon for the way in which our country
has contributed to the wars in other countries
that have produced so many refugees.
Christ have mercy   *Christ have mercy*

Lord, we ask pardon for our poor response to those asylum
    seekers
who sit in detention centres within our country
and for all those children, women and men
who will suffer from our government's policies.
Lord have mercy   *Lord have mercy*

South African Catholic Bishops' Conference
(adapted CAFOD)
South Africa/England

Missed Childhood

I was no latch-key kid,
We had no home.
Each day we left
The place we'd slept in,
Plastic bags holding our
Treasures, and we walked,
A leisured class,
Hopelessly killing time.
We looked at shops, and
Sat in parks, and
Waited to go inside.
I couldn't watch my mum
To learn her skills,
There was no space for
Creativity. I learnt
Survival,
Living's another thing.

Ann Lewin
England

The River of Hope

A Children's Liturgy

Fourteen children will each represent a country from which refugees have come to your country. There is no need for costumes of the country but they could be dressed in a plain pale coloured shift. They will each carry an object which refugees might bring from their homeland.

Close to the start of worship the children will come forward and say where they are from, what they have brought and place the object on a table at the front of the church.

I come from Zimbabwe. Everything my family owns is in this bag.

I am from Somalia. Mum said to bring the cooking pot because we always need to cook.

When we left Ethiopia, we brought our teapot so that we can have a cup of tea.

Before we left Eritrea, we got this visa for Australia.

We left our home in Bosnia in a hurry. Dad brought the photo album.

This scarf was embroidered by my grandma in Croatia.

In Serbia, we are very religious. This icon was the family's most precious possession.

My home was in East Timor. I left with nothing.

The Koran is our sacred book. We brought this with us from Afghanistan.

I come from El Salvador. This cross was painted by my uncle who is dead.

Girls in Sri Lanka wear beautiful scarves like this one.

As we left our home in Iran, we brought some bread for the journey.

Toys like this are popular in Iraq. It's the only thing I brought.

People in Nicaragua love music, so I brought my recorder.

Later, during the singing of a hymn, the children leave the church and return carrying a long piece of blue fabric. The fabric is wound

around the front of the church encompassing the table on which the
symbols were placed.

National Council of Churches
Australia

Cover Us With Your Wings, O Lord

Terror is at our heels.
Anxiety, uncertainty, vulnerability
Lie ahead.
We have fled to freedom.
And yet . . .
Our hearts are aching.

Response: Cover us with your wings, O Lord

Far from home.
Longing for the familiar.
A touch, a smile, a hug, a kind word.
Yearning to return.
And yet . . .
We must go forwards.

Response: Cover us with your wings, O Lord

Memories and dreams
Grief and hope
Death and new life
What might have been
What could be.
And yet . . .
Throughout
Remains
Your constant love.

Response: Cover us with your wings, O Lord

Margaret McNulty/CAFOD
England

At Worship

'Among those who went up to worship at the festival were some Greeks.' John 12.20

They came from a very different culture,
with its glorious art and its acropolis,
its philosophers and scholars,
its delight in human beauty
and its busy family of gods.

They came to worship at the festival,
with what intention?
To investigate a foreign rite?
To write their travel books?
Or to open their hearts
to new possibilities and a different holiness?

How thankful we are when those from
another country and tradition
join in worship with us.
Then we know, as never before,
That the gift of God is for all and forever.

Save us from coldness in our worship,
from the formality which never smiles,
and the granite tradition which has no room for change.
Help us to rejoice in enquirers
who ask awkward questions in strange accents,
so that together we may approach
the mystery of eternity
with humility and hope.

Bernard Thorogood
Australia

The Refugee

Some people disagree with the things I say
and do.
Sometimes I disagree with the way people
comment about refugees and where they
come from.
How about you put yourself in their shoes
and go through the things that they've
been through.
They struggle hard through poverty
they travel round with no belongings and
no money.
They put up with people calling them foul
names and they still walk
the main road of liberty.
Nobody knows their pain and how much
they have suffered and how long it has
taken them to get where they are in life.
Maybe, even if they haven't,
they still have a long lifetime to get to
where they want to be.
So before you decide to question them
and tell them where to go
just remember
They are humans like you and me,
but they're
suffering so physically and mentally.

Zola F.
England

. . . but understand

Ali is not my real name.
  These are not my people.
This is not my place of prayer.
  Yet, words that fall from strangers' lips
are welcome to my ear.
  In them I hear God speak.
I am refuge. Be not alone.
  I am strengthened, but understand,
I do not have joy.
  I do not have what you call, home.

Eve Jackson
England

On the Timor Sea

Under the tropical sun
the little, tattered fishing boat
made small headway,
the engine limping
and the swell lapping across the deck.

We sat cross-legged on the hatch
with our bundles and baskets of coconuts.
One day, two days, a week
and we were nearly there,
the long journey of escape nearly over.

Then the grey ship bearing down on us,
the loud hailer, the boarding party,
the roughness of armed police,
and our journey to a new prison.

Is this the way of your world,
  most gracious God,

that we journey from one prison to another?
Can it be wrong to seek freedom?
Are we criminals because we love life?

And I saw the new Jerusalem
with its walls and gates;
and its gates were always open wide,
and pilgrims went in and out freely
and found there the light of life.

Bernard Thorogood
Australia

walking wounded

all these wounded
walking around unseen
smiling faces
hiding broken hearts
broken bodies
never to be mended

rootless trees blowing
in the wind
crying silent tears
scarred like you and me
broken hearts
never to be mended

flightless birds
whistling in the wind
stumbling around unheard
coloured feathers hiding
broken bodies
never to be mended

stunted flowers
battered in the rain
tears mingling with rivulets
unseen, unheard,
truths unspoken
souls scarred for life

Naomi Young
England

Humane

Did you see the marine medic?
Chubby and bespectacled
holding the Iraqi child
traumatised by war.
Did you see the tender
puzzled look on his face?
The enemy whom he had come
to defeat and liberate.

We, onlooking, can only guess
at his bewilderment.
Cradling this wisp of humanity
caught in the crossfire of greed and cruelty.

If there are any rags of hope
to be gleaned from this benighted war,
it is in the image of a soldier
sitting cross-legged in the dust.
Vulnerable, ambivalent,
sharing the simplest of human needs
to touch, hold, be held.
Friend or foe?
Who is the vanquished now?

Wendy d Ward
Aotearoa New Zealand

To Nurture Conflict – A Recipe

Take equal measures of
youth
strength
intelligence
idealism
passion
goodness
beauty
love
courage
commitment
ambition
hope.

Bind together with
firm muscles
strong bones
eager eyes
fine brain
a beating heart.

Add some education.

Divide into two halves.

Into one half, knead love of country and a dash of despair. Leave to prove in a small container with curfews, checkpoints, closures, land confiscations, house demolitions, illegal settlements and forbidden roads. This will facilitate development of despair to counteract hope and fear to blend with courage, producing fanaticism.

Into the other half, knead pride in new nationhood, a dash of arrogance, further education. Leave to prove in an expanding container occasionally rocked by explosions. This will nurture fear and encourage multiplication of arrogance.

Leave both halves for long enough.

Then top the first half with foolish adult injunctions and a bomb. Remove from container but inject powerful memories of constriction and frustration. Top the second half with high-class military training and sophisticated weapons. Remove from container. Do not worry if this causes shaking and/or panic.

Place together at a border crossing or checkpoint and retire immediately.

Patricia Price-Tomes
Israel/Palestine/England

Happy Birthday, Baby Jesus

Happy birthday, baby Jesus,
    born in awkward circumstance,
named in heaven 'God is with us'
    while the world looked on askance.
You were praised by simple peasants,
    not by princes nor by priests.
Who should bring you priceless presents?
    Unbelievers from the East!

Son of Mary, girl unmarried,
    maid with soul who sang of peace,
with your father she was harried
    by the local thought police.
Boy delivered in a stable,
    tucked away behind an inn,
people libelled you with labels
    fixed by prejudice and sin.

Word of God for human reading,
    Holy Lord in fallen flesh,
one day you'll lie bruised and bleeding,
    cross stands waiting after crèche.

You confound all expectations,
        testing what we thought we knew;
deep Desire of all the Nations,
        exiles find their home in you.

Tune: Hyfrydol

Kim Fabricius
Wales/USA

Twenty-First Century Nativity
(Palestinian style)

Better not go to Bethlehem
her time is too near
the checkpoint no place
for labour pains
mothers die in childbirth
babies too
at the checkpoint
depending on the mood
of macho youth
soldiering with the IDF*

And if you do get through in time
where then?
not the Church of the Nativity
that's for sure
a corner in a shell-damaged house
with your shell-shocked relatives
the best you can hope for

Don't imagine either that
they'll let you return
you're curfewed in Bethlehem
long term
constantly vigilant
lest *your* home is next

* Israeli Defence Force

119

for the bulldozers
pray that you're out
when they come

Do you want him toddling
to the rumble of tanks
learning from his cousins
how to play soldiers
every now and then
losing one to a sniper's bullet?

Or consorting with angry lads
having fun
don't you know
they shoot kids who
throw stones at their tanks?

What next for him
university?
no choice naturally
but Bethlehem's good
nice campus nice chapel
Christian too
of course he may get
mixed up in politics
speak out for justice
share his bread with the poor
stand up for the oppressed
celebrate with sinners
the Israelis don't like
that sort of thing
it upsets them
who knows
what might happen then?

You're a sensible man, Yussef
don't go to Bethlehem.

Patricia Price-Tomes
Israel/Palestine/England

Homeless in Egypt

When people flee from scenes of war and carnage,
when people know terror because of violent rage,
where is the place of sanctuary?
When families are split by conflict,
when wounded victims escape from bloodshed,
where will they find a refuge?
Wounded Healer,
you inspire us to welcome the asylum seeker,
you encourage us to open our hearts and homes to the
    refugee.
When we offer sanctuary to such as these,
we open the door to the child whose family fled to Egypt.

John Johansen-Berg
England

Dog Roses
(Jewish Cemetery, Southsea, UK June 2003)

Cutting through side streets
I found, by chance

the small Jewish cemetery,
row on row of grey headstones;

loving sons and daughters
let down gently,

some as long ago as 1749,
on land leased for a thousand years.

Remembering how racists had
daubed paint, desecrated graves;

I stood staring through locked gates,
in strong sunlight.

Bitterness still blew here
on this hot June afternoon,

the band of scarlet dog roses
caught in the coil of barbed wire

which crowned the wall,
daring anyone to spur their flesh.

Denise Bennett
England

Reconciliation: Reality

Don't feed me with nice things
Don't tuck me in a safe bed
Don't kiss my wounds better
Don't pat me on the head

I have to be this LION
I need to ROAR and ROAR
I own this anger that bruises me
I'm wearing the shadow of war

Peace is not a sharing of the written word
Peace is not a given time or place
Peace begins with exploring the truth
              Inside our own quiet space.

Eve Jackson
England

122

Praying with Those who Weep

As you wept over Jerusalem, Lord,
    you weep over this troubled world tonight.

With you we weep in our hearts
    for all who are troubled and in deep distress
    for those who are anxious and afraid
    for those who are weak and ill
    for those who are facing death
    and those mourning the loss of loved ones.

With you we weep in our hearts
    for all who are unjustly treated
    for those misunderstood and wronged
    for those pushed to the margins of life
    for those whose humanity is denied by others.

With you we weep for all who suffer the horrors of war and
  violence
    for those whose lives have been torn apart
    for those who cannot forgive
    for those who have lost all trust in others.

As you wept over Jerusalem, Lord,
    you weep over this troubled world tonight
    you hear the cries of all your children and so
    we hold before you those close to us in this community,
    who need your healing, your encouragement, your love,
    to see them through difficult days.

We bring them all before you, compassionate Lord.
Amen

Wendy Ross-Barker
England

God Sees, God Suffers

In camps in Sudan and Rwanda
Your hands try and share out the grain
As a baby lies dying of hunger
Your stomach's distended in pain.

When a bomb goes off in a city
You cower in fear for your life
When a workman is kidnapped, then murdered
You wait and despair with his wife.

As a refugee from Uganda
You long to return to your home
As parents are brutally slaughtered
You hide, as an orphan, alone.

When a mine explodes in a rice field
You lose a foot and a leg
When a mother can't feed her children
You squat in the gutter and beg.

As Palestinians and Jews go on dying
You grieve for your land torn apart
As each of us breaks love in pieces
You bleed from a crucified heart.

Lynne Chitty
England

Goodbye, England

At the airport, someone in the queue
asks me, out of politeness, perhaps,
'Where do you come from?'
I try to answer,
though I don't want to tell my story all over again.
'I come from Zimbabwe', I say,

124

and before they ask more
I tell, repeating it like a lesson I've had to learn
my story.
I tell it without too much feeling.

They came for us
because we supported the Opposition.
They shot my husband dead in front of my eyes.
The little ones were screaming.
Then they seized my daughter,
my first born, Cynthia.
I don't know where they took her.
My mother came quickly with money.
She said, ' We will look after the children,
but you must go at once, tonight.'

I don't recall anything of the journey,
only when I arrived, the questions,
So many questions . . .
I could not answer them.
Afterwards someone told me
I was traumatised.

In my silly head I had an idea,
an idea of England and the English people.
I thought the land would be beautiful,
the people welcoming, warm and kind.
But the England I saw was ugly
and most of the people I met looked away.
Some of them hated me
and when, after all the months
of fear and loneliness and misery and bewilderment,
of filling in forms and going to court,
when they told me
'You must go back to your own country.
Your appeal against deportation has been refused,'
then I wanted to weep but my eyes were dry.

Now, at the airport,
the kind ones gather round me.
They are weeping now,
wordlessly holding and stroking me.
I want to smile,
to say 'thank you'
but there is too much fear,
too much disappointment,
too much terrible anger.

My eye falls on a scrap of plastic rubbish,
a crumpled sweet wrapper on the floor,
and I think,
I am like that, only fit to be thrown away.

Anthea Dove
England

He Broke the Rules

What a wonderful moment when Jesus reached through the
divisions that hold people back.

Jesus affirmed the woman at the well in a world that would
not treat women as equal;

he touched the 'untouchable' – reached out to the outcast,

broke through the barriers of racism, of class, of gender and
of caste.

This prophet was the great rule breaker.

He broke the rules that bind people and hold them back.

May we courageously follow this example and exclude no
one and welcome all.

May our churches be communities that welcome all and
  may we understand the deep joy of a gospel that nails our
  prejudices and human divisions to a cross of shame
and awakens us to a resurrection of community, love,
  equality and joy.

Garth Hewitt
England

Stations of the Cross in the Gulag

1. **A carpenter's son is condemned:** *no escape from history*

> A son looks up: intimate stars.
> Empty chairs, barracks in black snow,
> borders close. Secret police
> lock gates, stare. Fool's bells
> anoint his head: ring blood-bright.

2. **He takes a cross:** *a future is bisected*

> Circus tents are struck. He starts,
> off-balance – in two worlds.
> Congealing texts inscribe his back.
> Pain breeds fire: pinpoints
> eyes and his bastard play.

3. **He falls under its weight:** *a season for pruning*

> From the crypt, a last
> fugue beats his ears.
> Sages watch him, winter's
> prey, tumbling – top heavy
> on midnight's stage.

4. **His mother watches:** *a monotony of dying*

> She sings a cradle-lullaby for her
> crumpled child – many secrets,

private dreams. He rocks slowly.
Her silence says, 'Sleep quickly
now others swing the cradle.'

5.   **Another carries his cross:** *a city of one*

Another – ambushed and dark
in the sun's eclipse – drags linden
planks: sharp snow, flat antiphons.
The carpenter's son, lamed,
clowns on, impaled by a kiss.

6.   **His face is wiped:** *love reads the world*

She knew no answer; nor
guarded eternity, nor any
paradox; just lived day's reprise –
yet touched his eyes: scarlet
ribbons and exploding stars.

7.   **He falls again:** *a weight of mortality*

Unseen cargoes drive him down
to face the ghetto: grey flint, black
hail – neutral and indifferent.
Absence at this address: not like
Green Galilee or cranberry fields.

8.   **He sees women from the city:** *an epilogue for Jerusalem*

Mutinous houses. Bethlehem's
women come. Dig graves for new
children and native gods.
No hope now for hope's prince – nor
us, nor next year's larkspur.

128

9.   He falls for the third time: *scarecrows in Jerusalem's net*

Holiness and cold clogs slip
on iced flints. He seeks no applause
for shabby steps. They chant an
ad hoc requiem, dense syllables
draining the patience of secular air.

10.   He is stripped: *signals for atonement*

Each retina – specks of
infinity – shades nakedness
for its embrace of whittled
wood. At the rose window
ticket-holders wait: desire blood.

11.   He is crucified: *God is without God*

Drums hammer down the night.
Stars dry out. The canopy closes.
Carnival's king takes his throne.
Iron skies scream laughing-red
at such embroidery.

12.   He dies on his cross: *each death is new minted*

His tenancy ends with stained
amens. Grain is rolled,
wine stamped. Possibility ebbs
to nothing – still he rehearses
for an aubade.

13.   He is taken down: *cutting cards and mysteries*

From agony – or courtesy – pots
ask the potter: 'Why?' Dark-yellow
wisdom and its grammar declines ash,
not sense. Yet children still laugh, larks
sing and chestnuts ceremoniously bloom.

14.   He is put in a grave: *now will life mend?*

> Suns set crooked in this snow.
> Cafés close. Car parks empty. The band
> has gone. Return tickets are safe.
> Start back to ordinary places now –
> or stay for the aubade?

Derek Webster
England

Not so, this Christmas

Did shepherds once guard sheep
on hills near Bethlehem,
Fearing only wild animals?

Not so this Christmas –
when the danger that lurks in the hills is a camouflaged
   tank.

And were those shepherds made fearful
by bright lights which turned out to be angels
And a loud noise which became
a heavenly song to the glory of God?

Not so this Christmas –
when the sound in the sky is the roar of helicopter gunships,
the light, the bursting of a deadly rocket.

Did shepherds once walk freely
from those hills down to the town,
where folk slept soundly – apart from that group in the
   stable?

Not so this Christmas –
when the route is blocked by checkpoints
and a towering concrete wall,

and citizens, walled in, fear for themselves and for their
   children.

Is that family still there – poor, vulnerable?
Mother, father and the child
who will know suffering and sorrow and death,
yet through it all, bring hope.

People of God, go afresh to Bethlehem
In the light of reality.
Occupied then – occupied now
Innocents slaughtered then – and now.

Go and see the child who will grow
to be the man who cries for justice,
who dies to bring new life.

He invites us to follow him.

Wendy Ross-Barker
England

Refugee and/or Migrant Sunday

Pastoral suggestion

*For the Liturgy, have flags from the nationalities that make up the
community.*

Words of Welcome

Spoken by the Worship Leader or a migrant or refugee

Today we invite everyone to pray for refugees and migrants to
our country. Our worship is a celebration of the contribution
refugees have made to our community/country whose
population has a rich cultural mix. Many of us are refugees, or

the descendants of refugees, yet in recent years, some refugees have been targeted for abuse because of their country of origin and their beliefs. Sadly, there has developed a division within the community/country about policies on and treatment of asylum seekers.

Readings

Ecclesiasticus 3.17–20, 28–29
By being gentle and humble we will find God's favour.

Responsive Psalm: Ps 67.4–7, 10–11
This is a hymn of thanksgiving for God's goodness and care for the disadvantaged and poor.

Hebrews 12.18–19, 22–24
The new covenant is one of love.

Luke 14.1, 7–14
Jesus invites us to give without seeking a return.

A Reflection

Jesus uses a concrete situation to teach about humility and hospitality. God is not selective about who is invited to the table of the kingdom. An attitude of humility, of being receptive to God, will dispose us to act like God. We will recognise our duty to share what we have with the poor.

Places in the feast of the kingdom are for God to give as a free gift, not for us to take for ourselves as our right.

This teaching from Jesus concerning 'placement at the table' and 'hospitality' emphasizes important issues for us as we learn to live together and build our future together with people who are refugees, migrants and asylum seekers.

The Response in the Psalm clearly states that God has prepared a home for the poor. Can we listen to this challenge with the gentleness and humility invited of us in the first reading? Can we respond in the spirit of the new covenant to those seeking a place of safety? What if God has prepared this home for the poor in our community? Can we share our home, our table, without thought of reward?

The invitation is not to give up our homeland and our way of life, but simply to share it. The challenge is to recognise Christ in those who come, rather than determining with whom we will share our homeland.

Prayer of the Faithful

Any or all of the following could be added, keeping in mind the local community.

- For refugees: that God's presence will give comfort in their insecurity, and that our efforts will offer hope and bring justice.
  Lord, hear us.
- For all newcomers who have made this country their home: that they may find here peace, happiness and prosperity, and that we may all be enriched by the values, customs and cultures that we share.
  Lord, hear us.
- For all the people of this country: that we may have tolerance, openness and respect, so that we may welcome the stranger, offer support to those who have recently arrived, and give comfort to the homesick.
  Lord, hear us.
- For all of us: that we may change our way of thinking and be prepared to stop protecting our standard of living at the cost of developing nations and their peoples' quality of life; that we may live simply so that others may simply live.
  Lord, hear us.

Languages

In many communities there is a range of languages spoken. Some of these could be incorporated into the liturgy, always respecting its structure and balance. A reading could be read in another language, and the English translation included in a worship sheet or electronically. Some of the general intercessions could be translated into another language and prayed, so that all are engaged in worship, rather than listening to a concert. Invite the congregation to give the Sign of Peace to each other.

If this is the only time during the year that migrant groups celebrate their journey and life in the community, it would be appropriate to decorate and highlight the different shrines and statues with which the different groups identify strongly.

Place inserts in the church/area/parish newsletter on the multicultural composition of the local communities, with some stories of the experience of migrating, on present refugee questions in the world, and on the activity which could be a part of your mission.

Fr John Murphy
Catholic Migrant and Refugee Office
Australia
(adapted)

A Kind Thought for Asylum Seekers

In my experience it isn't often that a tolerant, informed, let alone Christian view is expressed about asylum seekers. I have a particular interest in this subject because I married an Iranian asylum seeker, who now has UK citizenship. His father worked hard to improve his family's income and status to the point at which they were able to move from a small, rural village to a more prosperous, middle-class life in Tehran. Here my husband received his university education and after his national service he set up his own pharmaceutical company. At this time in Iran many middle-class families sent their children to Europe to be educated. My husband's eldest sister had four boys, all of whom were educated at private boarding schools in England, thus contributing to our economy. At the time of the revolution she and her husband had to leave Iran because the work they had done in the days of the Shah was no longer acceptable. She moved to England to be with her sons, all of whom have now completed their university education here, hold well-paid jobs and are in no way a drain upon our economy. My husband stayed in Iran, but after a while his loyalty to the new regime was questioned and he was imprisoned and tortured. After his release he managed to arrange a business trip to Europe during which he decided to seek asylum rather than face the frightening prospect of an unknown and potentially dangerous future in his own country. He struggled for years to settle here but could not and has recently returned to Iran. Despite much personal discomfort, I feel compelled to write this to try to dispel some of the half-truths and myths associated with asylum seekers.

'ALL asylum seekers are spongers '
Whilst it is true that asylum seekers want some things that life in the UK offers – peace, safety and economic stability – all of the Iranians I have met here have been prepared to work hard to achieve these for themselves, and would have preferred to have been able to do this in Iran, without the upheaval and emotional distress of leaving their own country.

Sadly, my marriage failed. 'Well, what did you expect when you married someone like that?' How would YOU feel if you were in my, or my former husband's, shoes? He was young and successful, and had achieved more than he could ever have imagined. He had, by his own and his family's hard work, moved from a small, rural village to become a dynamic, well-educated and self-reliant businessman in Tehran. Then he became a social outcast in his wife's native land. I try not to be too judgemental when I encounter such hostility, but it is hard and painful to bear.

'It's a bad thing to be an economic migrant'
I know that my husband and other members of his family did not leave Iran primarily for economic reasons, but I ask you to reflect on the plight of those asylum seekers who do. Can you

135

put your hand on your heart and say that you would not try to get a better life for yourself and your family elsewhere if you were living in grinding poverty as well as under a harsh and oppressive regime?

I am not seeking to make a case for unlimited and unrestricted immigration, but merely asking for a more informed and tolerant approach to the many, who like my former husband, are faced with a daily barrage of political and media half–truths, hatred and ostracism, some of which is fuelled by racist attitudes. Such prejudice takes little account of their personal struggles or the important and valuable contribution which they seek to make to the economic, social and cultural life of their adopted country.

A kind thought, a word of encouragement to genuine asylum seekers, and where appropriate, a word of correction or challenge to those who oppose them would go a long way towards dispelling some of these myths.

It is a sad reflection upon many of the prevailing attitudes towards asylum seekers in our society that the author of these words feels the need to protect her family by preserving her anonymity. Think and pray on these things.

Anonymous

and accompanied by

No Place of Safety

Jesus said, ' Foxes have holes, and birds of the air have nests;
but the Son of Man has nowhere to lay his head.'
Matthew 8.20

Jesus, Son of God and Son of Man,
born in the dirt and stench of a stable,
laid in a makeshift cradle,
forced to flee from a ruthless, child-killing king;

Hear our prayers
for parents and children
who have no place of safety,
and nowhere to lay their head;
do not let us ignore them
when they look to us
for asylum and aid.

Jesus, Son of God and Son of Man,
wandering from place to place
as teacher and healer,
torn by the need to balance
engagement and withdrawal,
weighed down by the demands of the crowd;

Hear our prayers
for all who work alongside
asylum seekers and refugees,
and strive to raise awareness
of their rights and needs;
do not let us abandon them
to bear this burden alone.

Jesus, Son of God and Son of Man,
betrayed by a loveless kiss,
let down by one who had
boasted of loyalty,
nailed to a cross,
scorned and reviled
in the taunts of passers by,
laid in a borrowed tomb;
do not let us betray or deny you
when our discipleship
is put to the test.

Hear our prayers
for all asylum seekers and refugees,

when their suffering is ignored,
their dignity undermined,
their efforts dismissed or belittled,
their need exploited,
their rights denied.

Jesus, Son of God and Son of Man,
hear these prayers,
and call us to walk the way of your cross
as we strive to play our part
in answering them.

Jean Mortimer
England

Litany of Commitment for Human Rights Day
Excerpted from the Beatitudes (Luke 6.17–22 and Matthew 5.1–11)
and the Charter of the United Nations

Leader: God of all creation, we are your children. We are also the people of the United Nations.

People: **Help us to seek the security of the whole human family made in your image and for whom Jesus lived, died and lived again.**

Leader: Jesus said, 'Blessed are the peacemakers for they will be called children of God.'

People: **God of Peace, we your children and the peoples of the United Nations are 'determined to save succeeding generations from the scourge of war'.**

Leader: Jesus said, 'Blessed are those who hunger and thirst for righteousness' sake, for theirs is the kingdom of heaven.'

People:	**God of Love, we your children and the peoples of the United Nations 'reaffirm faith in fundamental human rights, in the dignity and worth of the human person and in equal rights of men and women and nations large and small'.**
Leader:	Jesus said, 'Blessed are you who are poor, for yours is the kingdom of God.'
People:	**God of life, we your children and the peoples of the United Nations will 'promote social progress and better standards of life in larger freedom'.**
Leader:	Jesus said, 'Love your neighbour as yourself and love your enemies, do good and lend, expecting nothing in return.'
People:	**God of Community, we your children and the peoples of the United Nations will 'practice tolerance and live together in peace as good neighbours'. We are called to be peacemakers to the Christ who came that we might know a peace that passes understanding. Lead us to rise up and be called children of God, citizens of a new world community. Guide us to speak boldly, with moral conviction, to the nations and to the world. Let us build, with your grace, a global community by acting now for world peace, for a flowering of justice, for an opportunity of love, for the realisation of Your peace. Amen.**

Presbyterian Peacemaking Program
Presbyterian Church
USA

No Cot for the Future
(A Liturgy)

Genocide in the sun: guns, shells, broken glass.
Annihilation today: black fields, broken cities.
Peace and justice: final illusions.
A tomb for the child: no cot for the future.

Litany

Our eyes have seen what may not be seen,
Our ears have heard what should not be heard,
Our hearts have felt what cannot be borne.
Such madness, Lord, such sorrow.

See prisoners torn and tortured, shocked and shot,
Hear victims, pinned, abused, misused, left hanging,
Remember those who dig graves for their own children.
Such horror, Lord, such horror.

For the hopeless – evicted, imprisoned, hopeless, mad,
For the helpless – harassed, resigned, despairing and sad,
For the neglected – sick, not clothed, not loved, not fed.
Such dread, Lord, such dread.

For those who love the earth and restore their planet,
For those who bring peace and love to their neighbours,
For those who refresh the world and love their enemies.
Such hope, Lord, such hope.

For the shining of the Father,
For the song of the Son,
And for the Presence of the Spirit,
Such thanks, Lord, such thanks.

Meditation

The commandment to love their neighbours brings Christians to the side of those who are crushed by the world. They join other men and women of good will and protest when religious fanaticism tears people apart and persecutes the unorthodox. They stand against ideologies which diminish by race, colour or affluence. They contend with economic structures which deprive people of their humanity. They resist the impossibility which haunts the lives of the crushed. The coinage of these rather abstract generalisations is this: Christians inveigh when a poor man starves, thirsts and is naked; when his wife is seized and raped by victorious soldiers; when small children are held in ignorance and burdened with labour; when his brothers and sisters are falsely imprisoned without hope; when his mother and father live with untreated disease and no medicines. Christians attend to the poor, the little, the forgotten and the impotent, those ignored by powerful sectional interests for one very precise reason. They see each person as an ikon of Christ. But there is more. Not only do Christians stand with those people who endure unmerited suffering, who cry for justice and freedom, they remember for love those who perpetrate these things. So they intercede very deliberately and thoughtfully for torturers, exploiters and oppressed, destroyers, liars and warmongers, that they may be disarmed by Love. For to remember only the weak and deserving is to do less than the Christ who asked that those who crucified him might be forgiven – and asked this as they were crucifying him.

A Prayer of Intercession

Lord, remember for love:
Those who wed poverty for truth's sake,
    The known St Francis . . . and the unknown;
Those who seek peace with an unending will,
    The known, Gandhi in India . . . and the unknown;
Those who draw the nations to unity and justice,

The known, Dag Hammarskjod . . . and the unknown;
Those who have wisdom to heal the body,
    The known, Alexander Fleming . . . and the unknown;
Those who sing songs of the soul for the poor,
    The known, Caedmon of Whitby . . . and the unknown.
Amen.

The Lord's Prayer

We, who know the pain of broken ties may say,
    Our Father.
We, who inhabit the ghettos affirm of you,
    Who art in heaven.
We whose names are remembered for abuse of Yours say,
    Hallowed be thy name.
We, who suffer brutality, discrimination and death, cry to
    you,
    Thy will be done on earth as it is in heaven.
We, who are refused the harvest of your land and sea, cry
    out,
    Give us this day our daily bread.
We give and seek compassion appealing
    Forgive us our trespasses
    As we forgive those who trespass against us.
We ask to be kept from what subjects others to us
    And lead us not into temptation
    But deliver us from evil.
We, without power, await the restoration of all things and
    say,
    For thine is the Kingdom, the power and the glory.

Save us, Lord, from those who think that they alone create
    Truth. Always their torture is to death.

Derek Webster
England

Seen in Ramallah

Automobile
metallic blue
trunk embellished
with tracks
of tank
thrust aside
worthless
rubbished
a corpse
in the road.

Patricia Price-Tomes
England

Our Only Salvation

O Holy One, we have made you
    'Lord Over All'
    the object of our worship
    our 'One True Religion'.
But our way is not your way;
You are self-giving love
    love that gives of itself –
    no self-serving attached.
You are this way made
    down-to-earth and human
    in Jesus of Nazareth.
You point the way
    not to Jesus as the founder
    of the only true religion
    but through him to
    your down-to-earth way
    of salvation – salvation for every
    earth-dwelling human;

You call us to choose self-giving love
in our self-serving world
of traumatizing terror
and twisted truth.
Through him you show the way
and the truth and the life of
self-giving love;
In this way you offer
our self-serving world
its only salvation.

Norm S. D. Esdon
Canada

Lament for an Olive Grove

olive
trees
grow not tall
and straight   but gnarled
curved   twisted,   softly clothed
in dainty   grey-   green leaves
age
beauty
wisdom
healing and
nourishment
are their song,
sharp appetisers
and   rich oil their fruit.

One day the
bulldozers came
crashing through   the
olive grove, destruction in their   wake
tearing up roots of our ancient   and
beloved trees our livelihood, and as we weep
our life drains away with their   sap.

144

Soldiers   stand guard over
the groves, over our stricken
mournful trees, their guns
menace us,   as we watch
broken hearted from afar.
Hope almost gone, we lay our plans, dangerous life-
threatening plans. At dead of night, the waning moon a faint
sliver in velvet black sky, we move slowly silently across the
sorrowing grove. Hearts in mouths, mustering every gram
of strength, praying that they sleep, we grasp the nearest
broken   corpse,   lift   it
shoulder high, and carry it
home, success lightening
our hearts a little as we lay
it safely down and take
our rest. Now craftsmen
are our hope, our only
hope,   for   sustenance
and survival. This holy
cross holds the story of a
sorrowing people; will you
buy it, will you stand with
us, speak for us, pray for
peace and work for justice?

Patricia Price-Tomes
Israel/Palestine/England

Singing, Praying and Holding Olive Branches

'I want the truth to be told, and my prayer is that peace might
come from the blood of my son.'

It was the mother of Johnny Thaljia speaking, a seventeen-
year-old Christian Palestinian boy shot dead in Manger Square,
Bethlehem, while holding not a stone or a gun, but his cousin's
baby in his arms. The family's shock and grief are tangible two

months on, and shared by the whole community, Muslim and Christian alike. We visited the Thaljia family on New Year's Day and asked what they would want us to tell people when we returned to England. Mrs Thaljia's reply needs to be heard and honoured.

There are signs of hope. On New Year's Eve we took part in a non-violent march for Peace with Justice, organised and led by all the Church leaders of the Holy Land. The previous night the authorities had tried to dissuade Bishop Riah (the Anglican Bishop of Jerusalem) from taking part and encouraging the walk. Two days before that a smaller march had been broken up with tear gas and a few days prior to that a peaceful march in Gaza had been fired upon.

In spite of this, on the last day of 2001 nearly two thousand local Palestinians and some Israelis were joined by six or seven hundred representatives from different countries. Together we walked – Christians, Muslims and Jews, singing, praying, holding hands and olive branches. We hoped to walk from Manger Square through the Israeli checkpoint into Jerusalem, and to circle the Old City praying for peace, justice and reconciliation. Messages of goodwill and prayers from all over the world were attached to balloons to be released at the completion of the walk.

A profound sense of friendship crossing barriers of faith, language and culture pervaded the crowd as we began walking through Bethlehem. There was shared pain and shared hope, even as we passed hotels and homes shattered by shells and bullets.

Over a mile before we reached the checkpoint three armoured vehicles blocked the road, with machine guns trained menacingly on the crowd. Led by the bishops everyone moved calmly and courteously towards the soldiers, stopped, and offered them olive branches of peace – Palestinian citizens with guns pointing at them, offering soldiers olive branches! It took nearly an hour of negotiation and assurance that there would be no trouble, before the soldiers finally agreed to let us proceed, but only as far as the checkpoint. 'Are you refusing us permission to pray in the Holy City for Peace?' the bishops had asked.

Of course the answer is yes. For tens of thousands of local Muslims and Christians are permanently banned from visiting their capital city for any reason at all, let alone to worship at their most holy places.

We walked on to the checkpoint where Christian and Muslim leaders led prayers and singing. Passages of scripture from Isaiah and from the Gospel resonated poignantly under the clear sky and the vigilant military cameras. Simply and clearly the leaders voiced our common call to end the occupation and to open Jerusalem to all.

The balloon messages were released, and as the crowds dispersed quietly, olive branches were once again offered to soldiers. Only the international visitors were granted permission to proceed into Jerusalem, where we were met near the pools of Bethsaida by several hundred Israelis who were planning to join their Palestinian brothers and sisters in a common witness for Peace with Justice. It is a cruel irony that such a powerful symbol of hope and reconciliation was denied by the authorities by the refusal to allow the peaceful marchers from Bethlehem and Jerusalem to join together. Once again the suffering of the present mingled with the hope for the future, as hundreds of Jews, Christians and Muslims prayed, sang and danced together, joined in spirit with all those who had been barred access.

Despite the size of the day's event, and the presence of numerous TV cameras and reporters, it all went largely unreported. Could this be because there was no violence to report?

Sadly it is true that the protection afforded the local people by the presence of international participants is not ordinarily available to the Palestinians of the West Bank. The following day we visited people whose homes and neighbourhoods have been shattered and destroyed by the bombardment of innocent civilians during the last fifteen months. The constant harassment, desperate economic hardship and effective imprisonment

147

of ordinary people in their villages tells a story still little heard and rarely acknowledged by the rest of the world. Some black South Africans recently visiting Bethlehem found the situation disturbingly familiar but even worse than in the darkest days of the apartheid years.

Despite all this we found a profound desire for peace in which both Israelis and Palestinians could share, and this even among those like Johnny Thaljia's parents, whose children have been brutally killed. But they rightly believe that peace without justice, and an end to occupation and apartheid, is no peace at all.

We only hope that international and church leaders might have the courage to support such a cry for justice which is the only way to a true and lasting peace.

Andrew Ashdown and Susan Sayers
England

Protecting the Persecuted

Call to Worship

Leader: There is no place where You cannot reach:
People: God who made the heavens and the earth.
Leader: There is no journey which You have not travelled:
People: God who shares our life in Jesus Christ.
Leader: There are no people beyond your care:
People: God who is the Spirit, the Comforter.
Let us worship God!

Leader: Let us 'gather into' our community of faith some of the people who are uprooted from their homes and countries around the world . . .

Suggested action by the congregation
The names of countries where there are known to be refugees or internally displaced people could be read and a symbol such as a flower, a poem or a picture could be stuck on to a display board or

altar cloth and linked to a world map with a ribbon. Candles could be lit.

Hymn – to be selected by the local church

Prayers of Adoration

Leader: Loving God, we give thanks that You care for all people but particularly the vulnerable and abused. We give thanks that You give some people the insight and courage to dissent, to act against cruel policies, to raise the hard questions to those in power and make us all rethink.

People: Loving God, thank you for the abundance and beauty of Your creation, meant for the enjoyment of all people. Thank you for the richness of different peoples and their cultures.

Prayers of Confession

Leader: Gracious God, we now bring before You our failings and omissions.

For those times when our fears, suspicions, avoidance of issues for fear of upsetting our family and friends or our lack of energy and action have damaged or estranged others.

People: Forgive us and deepen our courage and wisdom.

Leader: For not loving our enemies and not treating those who disagree with us with respect.

People: Forgive us and deepen our courage and wisdom.

Leader: For our failings – at individual, community and government levels – in generosity, compassion and imagination to devise better policies to assist refugees, asylum seekers and those in our immigration detention centres.

People: Forgive us and deepen our courage and wisdom.

Declaration of Forgiveness

All: We receive your gifts: forgiveness, healing, courage and wisdom.

Service of the Word

Suggested Bible readings with reflection:

Exodus 1.8–2.10	Resistance to persecution and unexpected allies in mercy
Psalm 124	God, the Protector of Refugees
Romans 12.1–8	Life in God's Service
Matthew 16.13–30	Peter recognises Jesus as Messiah

Hymn – to be selected by the local church

Sermon – to be according to local procedures

Hymn – to be selected by the local church

Affirmation of Faith

We worship one God,
In whose image all people are made,
Who calls us no longer to be strangers, but friends,
To whose service we are summoned,
By whose presence we are renewed.

Prayer of Intercession

For Our Nation and Leaders:

Wise and compassionate God, as a nation, help us to bear the burdens refugees and asylum seekers carry and not simply seek to shift the burden onto others.

Call our leaders to justice, generosity and compassion. Help them create and implement strategies that are fair and will benefit the . . . community and treat refugees and asylum seekers as human with dignity and care.

For Refugees:

O God, our comforter, we ask you to comfort the broken-hearted and protect the vulnerable. In places where violence destroys lives, bring your peace. In places where hatred disfigures communities, bring your love. God of justice, compassion, grace and mercy, hold back the arm of those who would do violence and wickedness. Bring down the proud and the powerful and lift up the downtrodden.

A Closing Prayer

Christ, our friend, when we were once distant strangers you proclaimed peace and brought us near. Help us to extend your grace and welcome in word and deed to all around us. Help us to live out the values you have called us to. Let us not be conformed to the world and behave with selfishness or indifference to the needs of others, but follow the way of your son who came not to be served but to serve. Let our lives and our words witness to your grace and love that reach out to the last and the least.

Hymn – to be selected by the local church

Blessing and Dismissal

God bless our eyes so that we will recognise injustices.
God bless our ears so that we will hear the cry of the stranger.
God bless our mouths so that we will speak words of welcome
    to newcomers.

God bless our shoulders so that we will be able to bear the
weight of struggling for justice.
God bless our hands so that we can work together with all
people to establish peace.

National Council of Churches
Australia

Strangers in a Strange Land

Globalisation has allowed money, services and commodities to
move around the world. But what about people? Famine, civil
war, racism, oppression and a lack of work drive people from
their homelands. It is not surprising then that the vulnerability around human migration is a key issue in contemporary
development theory and practice.

Nor is it surprising that this theme often emerges in Scripture.
The two great crises of the Old Testament, the exodus and the
exile, centre on this theme, as does the story of the Incarnate
Christ.

Joseph's family moves to Egypt to escape a famine, but as
time passes enslavement underlines their vulnerability. The
exodus is God's way of drawing the people of Israel back to
their home.

Much of the Law of Moses, drawing on this experience of
freedom from slavery, is rooted in an awareness of vulnerability. Time and again the Law reminds the people of Israel that
they may not do wrong to aliens.

Migrancy and vulnerability are even more central to the exile
in Babylon, which becomes a crucible for redefining Israel as
a religious community. The lament of those Jews taken into
captivity strikes a very contemporary note: 'By the rivers of
Babylon – there we sat down and there we wept when we
remembered Zion' (Psalm 137.1).

A third and perhaps most striking image is of the Holy
Family fleeing to Egypt to escape the wrath of Herod (Matthew
2.14). From the emotional high of the visit of the Magi, we can
only imagine the crisis into which Joseph, Mary and Jesus were
thrown by becoming refugees. But this sojourn in Egypt is a

powerful account of the connection between God-in-Christ and the vulnerability of so many of the world's migrant people.

Three important insights emerge as we allow these central biblical stories to throw light onto this experience of suffering.

The first is the awareness that the Bible engages with this kind of suffering, and that the revelation of God's word is found in the midst of it. God does not abandon those whose lives are shattered by such forced migration, but journeys with them and is found in the midst of their vulnerability. In Christ, God is as one among them, fleeing Herod with all his worldly belongings upon a donkey.

Second, though it seems hard to express it, the biblical witness reminds us that we cannot lose hope. From the depths of despair, of 'weeping when we remembered Zion', Deutero-Isaiah sounds the trumpet of hope as he announces the return: 'Those who wait for the Lord shall renew their strength, they shall mount up with wings like eagles, they shall run and not be weary, they shall walk and not faint' (Isaiah 40.31). Perhaps hope remains the last and yet most powerful weapon that the Christian faith can share in such times.

Finally, as the Law of Moses saw so clearly, there is an ethical command rooted in the experience of such vulnerability: The solidarity of God in the midst of such suffering together with the hope rooted in the gospel must find concrete expression in the hospitality extended by the people of faith towards the aliens among us. 'For by doing that, some have entertained angels without knowing it.'

Steve de Gruchy
South Africa

God of Compassion

Minister: I invite you to collect your thoughts as we take up our priestly role and turn to God to pray for the needs of the world.

Reader: *In ending the prayers please repeat the last phrase*

Let us pray for the Church throughout the world – for energy and commitment in her ministers and people to bring justice and the hope of Christ to traumatised, frightened and displaced people.

Pause *for reflective prayer*

God of Knowledge, hear us.

All: **God of Knowledge, hear us.**

Reader: Let us pray for political and social leaders – that understanding the desperation and fear that forces people to leave homes, families and ways of life, may bring compassion and common sense to the process of their integration into a new country.

Pause *for reflective prayer*

God of Understanding, hear us.

All: **God of Understanding, hear us.**

Reader: Let us pray for our country – for greater opennness in those born in ..... to the enrichment of our culture when we welcome and include people of different origins.

Pause *for reflective prayer*

God of Wisdom, hear us.

All: **God of Wisdom, hear us.**

Reader:	Let us pray for own community – that we may reach out with Christ's hands and heart to befriend and support newcomers, the lonely and the traumatised.

Pause *for reflective prayer*

God of Compassion, hear us.

All:	**God of Compassion, hear us.**

Minister:	Lord, no one is a stranger to you and no one is ever far from your loving care. In your kindness watch over refugees, migrants and exiles, who have left home and familiar customs and ways. Bring them safely to a place where they belong and help us always to show your kindness to strangers and those in need.
	We make these and all our prayers through Christ our Lord.
	Amen.

Helen Coleman
Aotearoa New Zealand

Holy and Liberating God

Holy and liberating God,
you revealed yourself
as the one who saves people from slavery.
You gave the law that we should worship you alone
and not worship gods of metal.
We confess that we have trusted our safety
and security to gods of metal
that we create to kill and to maim.
Lord have mercy
Lord have mercy

155

Holy and hospitable God,
you revealed yourself
as the one who cares for the refugee
                    and the homeless.
We confess that we have been indifferent
to the plight of those who come to our shores
seeking safety and security.
Christ have mercy
Christ have mercy

Holy and compassionate God,
you reveal yourself
as the one who hears the cry of the poor.
We confess that our wealth and consumption
is at the expense of those who have nothing.
Lord have mercy
Lord have mercy

Holy and merciful God,
you reveal yourself
as the one who always
recalls humanity to yourself.
We come before you in confidence,
trusting that you will restore us to right relationship
with you and each other.
We give thanks that we are a forgiven people.
Thanks be to God
Amen.

National Council of Churches
Australia

Ruth (2)

My man is dead now, so where must I go?
Women are nothing but chattels and sheep;
Herds of us trotting close after our men.
My man is dead now, so where shall I sleep?

Where do I go now and where do I stand?
Back to my mother and my mother's gods,
Or wander with his mother, back to her land,
Trusting her God against all of the odds?

What is there for us wherever we go?
Flocks of us following men-folk around,
Hoping for grains on a winnowing floor,
Grazing for grace on the dustiest ground.

What may we hope for wherever we roam?
Kind gods to choose us from out of the flock?
Good men to pen us and find us our food,
Elevate us to breeding stock?

Lucy Berry
England

4

Living on the Edge

I was naked and you gave me clothing,
I was sick and you took care of me.
Matthew 25.36

Vulnerability is the keynote of living on the edge. Many people,
because of who or what they are or the way in which they aim to
live their lives as they have been created to be, find themselves
ostracized and often bullied by members of society. People who
are creative, people who live outside the accepted 'norm', are
frequently undervalued and disregarded as valuable members
of communities. They are vulnerable people. Society is intoler-
ant. The person who speaks out against injustice, the homeless
person because of sad and difficult circumstances, the *Big Issue*
seller, the gay person, the depressed person and people with
mental health difficulties, the child, young person or adult who
prefers not to 'be a part of the crowd', know very well what it
means to be living on the edge.

An anonymous person has contributed 'Accepting Who "I
Am"' (page **173**). 'Despised – Rejected – Crucified' (page **177**)
is a very telling piece written by Norm Esdon of Canada.

Lord of This Day

Lord of this day and of our whole life
thank you that each day
we can change our ways to your way.
Thank you for the people we have met today;
those who challenge how we think;
those who accept us as we are;
those who forgive us.
Thank you that their response to us
helps us to accept ourselves and others
and to find new ways to love our neighbours and ourselves.
Amen.

Corrymeela Community
Northern Ireland

God Search

We seek God in our most familiar places,
within the comfort of the known and true
among the safest and most friendly faces,
where we know best what we should say or do.

We find God in the most unusual places,
waiting for us among our lowest days;
smiling at us from unexpected faces;
following down our dangerous, wanton ways.

Throughout the world God knows our human faces,
feels every pain and calls us by our names,
forgives our sin, as in his holy places
he bears the cross built by our human shame.

God finds us out in all our secret faces,
knows what we do and where we hide away,

161

calls us to follow him to unknown places,
and through his love helps us to find the way.

Colin Ferguson
England

Bless All Those Who Come in Anger

Gracious God,
Bless all those people who come in anger to our cathedrals
and churches.
Angry with us, angry with the world, angry with you, angry
with themselves.
Teach us the hard truth that they are not disrupting our
worship with their outbursts but contributing to it honestly
and urgently.
When we are uncomfortable and wish they would leave,
rebuke us and show us how to listen and change as well
as challenge and uphold. Enable us to love ourselves and
you, that we may honour all who come and not miss the
glimpse of you they have to share.

Lynne Chitty
England

Get On With It

Get on with it and go to those,
to those who need you most,
and bigger questions, they will wait,
you're needed at your post.

Get on with it, for death will wait,
you have a life to live.
Look all around to those in need,
you have so much to give.

Get on with it, look straight ahead,
the present beckons you;
for in this place and at this time
there's much for you to do.

Get on with it. Yes, go with God.
Yes, go to all the earth,
and in your living and your love
mark everybody's worth.

Andrew Pratt
England

Boxes

aren't they pretty little boxes
the ones they keep us in
neat and square and stackable,
everything fits in
not me
I don't want your nice, neat
symmetry
your Ikea practicality,
your Homes & Garden's conformality
and placid status quo
I don't want your idea of fashion
because you have no passion
and my idea of independence
is not a piercing through my nose
yes, they're pretty little boxes,
wood and glass and lacquer,
ornamental and efficient,
from office chic to
tupperwared kitchen
it's good to collect boxes
they have their uses
I can see

but they're not so good for people
don't you want
to be set free?

Naomi Young
England

We Didn't Think

We didn't think
you'd be interested.
We didn't think
you'd want to join.

We didn't think
you'd want to come.
We didn't think
you'd mind.

We didn't think
you'd go without saying
Goodbye.

We didn't think.

Christine Ractliff
England

Not the Last Word

It feels as though all that I've given
Is being thrown back in my teeth.
Those years of effort, care and dedication
Evaluated in that one chill word,
Redundant.
But though they have decided
They can do without me,
I do not accept the label, failure.

My value does not lie in cost-effectiveness
But in experience, skills, talents;
I am me.

I'm not redundant, I'm available.

I hope to God that's true.
Right now I feel as though
I'm at the crucifixion,
Crying in agony
Why have you let me down?
There were no guarantees then,
Were there, that there would be
Resurrection.

Ann Lewin
England

On the Edge

The theme for One World Week was 'Living on the Edge'.
Ecumenical worship had been planned. It was to take place in
the cathedral. The organisers of the service were keen to use
appropriate symbols. A number of people had been asked to
come with an article expressing the theme. They would carry
them in procession and place them in a prominent position
to form a display. Another bright idea had been to ask that a
vendor of the *Big Issue** be invited to stand at the entrance to
the cathedral, selling his magazines – a living example of the
theme. It was a grey and blustery afternoon. The vendor stood
there as members of the churches made their way in to take part
in the worship.

'Have you sold many?' I asked, holding a copy of the same
edition, bought earlier in the week, which I had intended to
carry in the procession. He seemed very depressed. Most
people were ignoring him. He said that having been asked to

---

* *Big Issue* is a weekly magazine sold by homeless people on the streets of
London and other cities and towns in the UK.

come, he had bought a bundle, hoping to sell them. Now he would be 'out of pocket'. Vendors have to pay for their supplies before benefiting from those they sell.

I went inside and expressed concern to the organisers of the service. They shared my concern and wondered what to do. Why not bring him inside and invite him to take part in the procession? He agreed. He told me a little about his life, how he had come to be homeless and how he longed for something better. Coming into the cathedral was a strange experience for him and took some courage. I walked with him in the procession and he sat beside me during the service. Towards the end it was clear that he was becoming restless. There had not been much that made sense to him. 'Why not go outside now?' I suggested, 'and I shall try to encourage people to buy from you as they leave the cathedral.'

He sold a few more then but not enough to make it worth his while. The organisers promised that they would arrange for him to be reimbursed.

I hoped that they would not forget all about it as they moved on to consider next year's theme.

Wendy Ross-Barker
England

A World Out There

There's a world out there
of hurting, hurting people.
And here in church we
think we've so much to offer,
but we don't reach them,
because we don't understand
or because we don't want to understand.
It's safe in here.
We can pretend there's no hurt,
that everyone is like us.
Good upright Christian people.

And I'm hurting too,
because I don't want it like this.
I want to be a minister in a church that cares,
that's open and welcoming and loving
where all can come in
whatever their past.
And not be judged, just loved.

That's the church I want to be part of,
Prepared to hurt too,
Prepared to fight
Prepared to shout
For justice, for freedom, for dignity, for pride:
      in being human,
      in being loved,
      in being unique,
      in being created by God.

A church that is prepared to shout from the rooftops –
'The way things are is WRONG.'
We want a better way.

Lord, it hurts to try and bridge this divide.
To be torn in two.
Trying to be what the church wants me to be.
A minister created in their own image.
Leading worship, visiting, chairing meetings,
raising money to mend the church roof
while out there is a world in need.
A world in need of You.
A world in need of love and care.
A world in need of being made whole.
And it can't be whole unless it has You in it.
Unless people are whole – body, mind and spirit.
Finding homes, jobs and food for their souls.
Desperate, desperate needs.
And we discuss performing rights licences,
electrical wiring and Christmas carol concerts.

Lord, is this what You want of me?
How do I make them see?
There is none so blind as those who will not see.
How long, O Lord? How long?

And I'm in trouble
because I don't attend harvest suppers.
While 'out there'
people are telling me they are going to kill themselves
because there's no other way,
no other point.
What is the church about?
So insular
so out of touch.
Does Christ still say
'Why, oh why, have you forsaken me?'
And we, the church, stand, condemned.
And I'm a part, yet not a part, of it.
Torn and battered.
O God, give me strength.
For I can do no other.

Jenny Spouge
England

Not that Easy

My first reaction
on reaching the ward
was one of
pure breath-stopping panic.
This wasn't a ward
in which you recovered
it was a place
where you waited to die.

No-one spoke
no-one was able to.

The only sound was moaning
or occasional 'Oh God'
and the lady in the corner bed
looked like she was praying.

I went to the bathroom.
Dirty clothes and bed linen
lay in the base of the shower
urine seeped from them
and now covered the floor.
I walked through it slipping by the door
and my slippers were wet.

The next day
a priest was brought
to the lady in the corner bed.
They prayed urgently together.
Her son told me
she longed for death
but said bitterly
'It's not that easy to die'.

I went home on the third day.
I looked around
and said goodbye
but no-one answered.
They didn't realise I'd been there.
I threw my slippers in the bin
on the way out.

Jayne Greathead
England

Mobility Allowance
(for Jayne)

Last week I felt well enough
for a train trip to town,
my first in years.
I planned it for hours,
I timed my snail's pace
and arrived on the platform just right,
with all the normal people.
We were standing around.
I can't usually say 'we',
but that day I could.
I had a glimpse of everything
I've got used to not having.
It was a perfect day.

As the train was coming in
I had a sudden urge
to throw myself in front of it.
That wasn't despair.
I wanted oblivion,
oblivion in that moment: I felt –
on the fringe of beauty.

It lasted for a few seconds,
but I meant it.

Geoffrey Herbert
England

Let Her Go Hungry

On Corpus Christi we celebrate the Bread that is broken for
   all.
You only have to come to feast as the five thousand feasted.
With twelve baskets of bread left over, there really is plenty
   for all –

Enough for You, whoever You are, if you are willing to
come.

Were you there at that feast with the 4999?
Were there Jews? Were there Arabs? Were there blacks?
What about men who love other men – the centurion who
loved his male servant?

And what about me? Would I have been fed?
An unwelcome child in my mother's arms, a lesbian,
conditioned to be second best.
Would Jesus have said:
'Hey, don't give any to that woman there, the one with the
now happy smile.
She shouldn't be treated the same as the rest. Let her go
hungry.'

Sarah Ingle
England

Gay Child Speaks

I have loved you all my life
And you have loved me back
With lurking reservations
For all those things I lack:

I do not have the children.
I do not have the spouse.
I do not feel the kind of love
You did when you kept house.

So, could you *try* to love me
For all the things I *have;*
The brave, lone vulnerability
Of my own kind of love?

The unmapped, stony pathway
You never had to walk –

171

And listen to your baby
Now I have learned to talk.

Please want for me the love I need
And, perhaps, give it too,
So I may feel that I belong
In my world – and with you . . .

Lucy Berry
England

Exile of a Gay Man
(Ezekiel 12.1–6)

Dig through your wall
so that you're unsafe
and people will ask *What are you doing?*
– something crazy and alone.

Heave up your baggage
put it on your back
feel its weight
lumpy ingots of darkness.

Cover your face
you won't see what you're leaving
no one will see you're grieving.

Go into exile
where you don't belong.

You don't belong.

Geoffrey Herbert
England

Accepting Who 'I Am'

As a babe
restless – rejecting human love
yet much adored.

When under-five
fun-seeking,
invariably defiant,
no time for dolls or pretty clothes.

At school –
from being withdrawn, apprehensive,
(tearful even)
to becoming crafty and creative.

In adolescence, turbulent,
refusing to conform,
though socially mature.

As rebellious student,
exploring human sexuality,
reverently accepting who 'I am'.

Time to 'take your partner',
experience adulthood –
living life on the margins of society.

Now – praying; working for change,
committed to inclusiveness,
to positive new ways of being church –
hopeful, trusting, caring and fulfilled.

Anonymous

Three Kings

Two thousand years ago there was
pain, there was
birth, there was
joy. There also were
three kings.
Last night there were
three kings, their offerings unsung,
who shone before their Lord:
a nurse, a paramedic,
a houseman exercising hands,
all bowed over a trolley.
No star to guide
but a neighbour's need.
Their gifts – themselves.
Their talents saved an unwed mother's life
and gave the world a son.
Three kings.
Three kings who put the bat-black night
to flight
and set a world of new-born love alight.

Harry Wiggett
South Africa

Window of Hope

Silence, only my thoughts shouting in this empty place,
Alone, in a building built for an army of chaos, now empty
    and
lifeless, plain neutral walls, ceiling and fittings,
bright lights casting not a single shadow on the spotless
polished floor.

Hope stretched to despair, questions of why long gone,
Staring into the stained-glass window, my 'window of
    hope',

bright colours out of place, its ten-foot stature reduced to insignificance in this clinical wilderness, separated from those I love by the situation.

Thomas, nine weeks old, only four days at home,
Gasping for air in the tiny lung, working alone, doing the job
of two, hindered by pneumonia, infection . . .
Oxygen, resuscitation, ventilation.

Tonight I cannot spend with him.
The machine's pipes and the white uniforms too much to bear.
Thoughts of being prepared for what might be,
Inert, unable to scream. Unable to cry.

Thoughts of Danielle, five years old,
the excitement of her new brother destroyed,
the family she loves dismembered;
Of Joseph, three years old, confused, no longer coping,
passive, disturbed by events;
Of Clare, my strength, worn to breaking point,
trying to cope apart. Never before has anything threatened
our bond of gold. And myself, drawn to Thomas by love,
obsessive to the point of destroying all, all I am, all my
dreams,
all my love. Feelings that have lasted all night, all week.

The conclusion: a meeting with Clare over breakfast,
a joint decision, taken against advice and better judgement:
We take Thomas home to be part of his family,
caring together for his fragile life,
rebuilding our own.

And now? Thomas, four years old, is running down a field
with Danielle, Joseph and little Luke.

A miracle for sure. Full of energy. Full of Life.
As me and Clare reminisce on that lonely time, the strength it
has given us all.

Michael
England

the silence carrier

the silence carrier
carries at all times
a special

space

for others to fill
a worry a trouble
a thought is spoken
and drip by drip words
that could have filled a
pool of sorrow to the brim
can now be poured away
so that no-one need
ever drown from
loneliness

Eve Jackson
England

Soil

He came to me last night and said
This time I tell you: I want a 'boy'
I trembled and shivered within myself
How can I say a word to him

Am I a God or holy being
Who knows all hidden plans?
But I know, my worth in his eyes
Is a disposable object or thing
The fear of life crept in me once again

I looked at mother earth and nodded
I will feed her once more the fruit of my womb
Or may I attain the courage to die.

Sr Nasreen Daniel
Pakistan

Despised – Rejected – Crucified

I am betrayed and deserted
    by those who profess
    to understand me
    support me
    love me
I am misunderstood
    by father and mother
    sister and brother
I am denied
    by my closest friend
I am scourged
    by the absolutely certain
    of even my own religion
I am condemned
    by Capitol & Temple
    secular & sacred
    foe friend and family
I am despised – rejected – crucified
    for saying and being
    who I am
        I am The Outsider

Yet I feel
   attended and directed
   through the charcoal night
   outside the margins of
   the communal fire
I am embraced and empowered
   through my night-blackened cross
to roll away
   fear and self-pity
and come out
   of my whitewashed tomb

I am not alone – the Wise and Holy One
   welcomes me
   walks with me
   blesses my own
   I-Am-Who-I-Am

Norm S. D. Esdon
Canada

Depression

I am the monster cloud
Who rests on your shoulders,
Filling your mind with dark
Insistent whisperings:
'You are nothing, no one.
No one needs you.
See how they turn their heads
From your tears,
Thinking that, maybe, whatever ails you
Serves you right.
Lose yourself in me.
No one will miss you.'

Christine Ractliff
England

Thomas, Thomas

Thomas, Thomas, stop your doubting
Feel these wounds and then believe!
Ease for each new generation
Doubt in things we cannot see.

Speak to all our fear and longing.
Speak to Jesus in our place.
See the proof that we are seeking.
Long to meet him face to face.

Thomas, help us feel his presence
In the broken bread and wine.
May we each in turn be touching
Pieces of the realm divine.

Thomas, Thomas, stop your doubting
Feel these wounds and then believe!
Ease for each new generation
Doubt in things we cannot see.

Michael Jacob Kooiman
Canada

Like a Child

I sit in human silence,
the bright day in my lap,
expecting to receive a goodness
that I have not earnt
and cannot buy.
But in innocence
my heart and hands are opened
in readiness; like a child
waiting in line
for a face to shine upon me.

Eve Jackson
England

A Story from Samaria

Narrator: He had no bucket and the well was deep,
He was a stranger, stranger than she guessed.
And while the village dozed in noonday heat,
He sat beside the well and took a rest.

She had no husband and her life was hard.
Five times a widow, many times abused.
He was unmarried and a foreigner.
Their conversation cut across taboos.

Jesus: 'Give me a drink.'

Woman: 'Why are you asking me?
Your race and mine may share no cup or jar.'

Jesus: 'Water's God's gift, eternal-springing water.'

Woman: 'Then give me some and I will thirst no more.'

Jesus: 'Go fetch your husband.'

Woman: 'Stranger, I have none.'

Jesus: 'That's true. Of all the men who've shared your bed,
none now protects you.'

Woman: 'Since you know so much,
since you're so clever, tell me, Where is God?'

Jesus: 'Not on this mountain where you praise God's name,
nor where God's temple stands on Zion's brow.
God shall be praised in Spirit and in Truth.'

Woman: 'Sure, when Messiah comes!'

Jesus:	'He is with you now.'
Narrator:	He asked for water and she raised her head.
	He offered water and she raised her eyes,
	He recognised her without condemnation.
	She saw him, in the silence of a surprise.
	She drew no drink for him, but left her jar,
	And hurried back, despite the noonday sun.
Woman:	'Can he be the Messiah, after all?
	This man, who's told me everything I've done'
Narrator:	But that was long ago. Race still divides,
	And water's short and broken wells run dry.
	Sitting there in the heat to beg a drink
	Did more for peace than all their warlike cry.
	When miracles no longer are believed in,
	And hate has poisoned hope, the future's bleak.
	Is it only when an outcast meets Messiah
	That Palestinians and Israelis speak?

Barbara Moss
England

You See Our Prejudices

You see our prejudices.
Transform them into
eyes of curiosity.
You see our ignorance.
Transform it into
a sensitive enquiring mind.
You see our misinterpretations.
Transform them into
laughs that break the tensions.
You see our differences.

Transform them into
tables loaded with a multitude
of food and drinks.
You see our fear.
Transform it into
a fervent united song.

Per Harling
Sweden

Where Is Love?

Jesus said: As I have loved you, so you must love one
another.

When we see divisions in families,
        in friendships,
                in communities –
Where is love?

When in the wider world we see enmity,
        hatred,
                cruelty –
Where is love?

When we use a hasty word,
        are thoughtless,
                forgetful,
                        wounding –
Where is love?

When we are put down,
        put out,
                forgotten,
                        wounded –
Where is love?

Christine Ractliff
England

From the Other Side

I had never expected to be on the other side. I had arrived before, a new person to established communities, but always to a warm welcome, friendliness, acceptance. I had never before experienced rejection, deliberate unkindness, cruelty even – and suddenly that was the picture of my life just at the very worst time. But a wise friend, many years later, showed me that those who treated me so unkindly had been my angels in disguise. Without them, I might not have survived.

My about-to-be-bankrupt husband had committed suicide and I, in the bewildering trauma of bereavement, had also lost my home – I'd guaranteed all his debts. I was shocked, numb, and terrified that I'd end up as one more homeless statistic sleeping in a box on the streets somewhere. This was Thatcher's Britain.

Then I got a job – it seemed the perfect job! And a friend offered me a room in their house so I could move to London and take that job. I leapt at the chance, said goodbye to all my friends, packed my last few possessions and headed off for the big city, filled with hope.

What followed was a catalogue of disasters. The job turned out not to be quite what it had appeared to be – and as for the people, for a start I was forbidden to admit that my husband had committed suicide. In fact, it seemed I had to hide just about everything about myself – not easy when the PR department are interviewing you for a profile! For weeks, I felt ashamed to be me, dishonest with my new colleagues, always afraid something might slip out and bring the house of cards crashing down on me. In the end, I knocked it down myself and told the whole truth. And that was the beginning of the end with that job. I lasted less than six months and quit.

My new base developed into an affectionate relationship and I had hopes of a new family, new social circle, new life – there is such strong biblical support for new beginnings! The price was that I must not weep or grieve, must not mention my late husband's name – and must not take exception to the flock of proprietorial women who appeared to have prior claims on my

183

new partner and were determined to prove it. It was a high price for a roof above my head.

I hastily found myself a church. The initial welcome was warm and I breathed a sigh of relief. Refuge! But then quite innocently I managed to offend one of the congregation who waged such a campaign of spite that I searched for ways to avoid attending on Sundays, ways that would not hurt the lovely members of the congregation who had been kind to me. And the best way, as a lay preacher, was to get out and fill the very many empty pulpits of Greater London.

A large proportion of the widows and widowers of suicides themselves commit suicide within a few years of their loved one's death. My angels in disguise prodded me into staying alive. Every unkindness, every disaster generated a reaction that kept me alive – albeit angry! And much more understanding of what it is to be on the other side.

Dorothy Stewart
England

Keeping Faith

She didn't do picnics, parties,
days at the seaside.
She never attended school plays,
or prize-givings
or took her small daughter
who ached for words
to the library.

On Boxing Days
she packed her off to the pantomime
with the neighbour's kids
and every Sunday
bundled her to the Baptist church
while she downed her Wincarnis
and valium in between cooking the roast,
trying to pick herself up.

184

At Sunday School her daughter
learnt about Elijah, saw bible slides;
the stoning of Stephen,
the parable of the Good Samaritan.
At Christmas she queued to be an angel.
Here she was taught obedience
to honour her mother;
to sing *Give me joy in my heart* . . .

and gradually
she learnt to accept her mother's sickness
brought on by the fever of war
and widowhood;
to deal with her wildness,
the voices in her head;
to bite her lip when she cursed . . .

And fifty years on,
every Friday she takes
her mother's frail hand, leads her
to the tearoom. They share cake;
she brings her gifts of sweets and soap
but they do not kiss.

Denise Bennett
England

Life's Lesson

You of the gentle touch and limitless devotion,
You, Mother in a million, strong and bold;
The rock who always shouldered every burden,
The harbour in life's storms, the anchor's hold.

The bravest of the brave in times of trouble,
Upholder of God's word, unending love;
You taught us to respect His will and wisdom
Accepting all the things we could not *prove*.

Now you are old, your mind all dark confusion,
Accepting this is more than I can bear;
And yet, your gentle wisdom still upholds me
Your smile still tells me *He is there*.

I ask him why it is that you should suffer,
Why does he wait so long to take you home?
You, dear one do not question your condition,
You simply say with love, 'Thy Kingdom come.'

And as for me, I see, although I've *lost* you,
In that your mind's no longer free,
Your body has to stay until He's ready,
And waiting is His way of teaching me.

Nia Rhosier
Wales

Home

I left along a broad, high corridor.
Large windows, at the end, were very bright.
And there she stood, against the morning light,
Leaning beside, (I thought), her bedroom door.
She seemed almost translucent; frail and thin
With colours which she wore all mixing in.

A lilac knitted cardigan,
Jaunty child's sun-hat in appalling green,
A pin-tucked sensible Viyella blouse
Above a perma-crease pink kilted skirt.
And Wellingtons. (Off to the beach? Perhaps).

'Hello', I said.
'Hello. Do I know you?'
'Well, no.' I said. 'I don't believe you do.'
'What are you doing here?' she asked.
'Just visiting. I must go now', I said.

186

By that her old-young face was changed.
Old now. And trembling.
She took off the hat.
And in a tired voice,
Both clear and here,
(Far too aware), said:
'Yes. And how I wish I could do that.'

Lucy Berry
England

Semi-Sheltered
Reflections on adjusting to less independent living

The retirement flat is classified as 'semi-sheltered'
and this is indeed how it feels to me,
a half-way house in which to pause
and adjust my pace on the journey
towards acceptance of old age.

The gardens are spacious yet secluded.
Mature trees grow in abundance
around its borders,
providing privacy and shade.
I can place pots and tubs in the courtyard
or plant up one of the borders
to maintain the illusion
of still being a gardener
without too much effort or pain.
Someone else cuts the grass!

There is a security entrance system
and a closed circuit camera
linked to my television set,
so I can see who is calling
before opening the door.

A resident House Manager
will check on my well being

every day if I request it,
and there are emergency cords
to summon help when needed.

There is a communal library, lounge,
kitchen and laundry room,
where books can be borrowed,
weekly coffee and conversation enjoyed,
afternoon tea and sympathy dispensed,
or the world put to rights
while the laundry is done.

There is a lift
for those who can no longer
manage to climb stairs.
The Access Bus comes on Thursdays
to provide transport
for a supermarket trip,
but I still drive my car
and force myself
to ascend to my flat on foot,
except on really bad days.

I like the security and relative ease,
but sometimes it feels too much
like being on holiday, alone
in a comfortable, convenient,
yet strange hotel!

I miss the freedom
of my own little garden,
coming and going
as I please through my own
front and back doors,
without the restriction
of having to remember
to tell the House Manager
when I intend to be away.

My family are relieved
that I have made this move.
My head tells me it was
the right thing to do,
but my heart still misses
my former home and independent life.
So I am only semi-content;
glad that they know I am safe,
but sad and not yet fully adjusted
to this semi-sheltered state.

A Prayer

Eternal God, in whose house
are many dwelling places,
help me to make
this half-way house my home.
Grant me good humoured acceptance
of the restrictions and frustrations
of growing old.
If I 'rage against the dying of the light'
and vent my anger in inappropriate
or misdirected ways,
give me the grace to remember
that I have a permanent home
in the shelter of your love.

Jean Mortimer
England

At Eighty-One

At eighty-one I've learnt to surf the net.
I didn't really think what this would mean.
Found a haunting picture I can't forget.

The tutor said, 'just click' see what you get,
my own face stares from the computer screen.
At eighty-one I've learnt to surf the net.

As a prisoner of war I feel regret
to see me – and three comrades looking lean.
Found a haunting picture I can't forget.

I hadn't known this shot was taken, yet
here's Harry, John, Len and me, snap not seen.
At eighty-one I've learnt to surf the net.

Brutalised, beaten, a half-starved quartet;
three of us survived, John died aged nineteen.
Found a haunting picture I can't forget.

Strange to discover that my cheeks are wet;
the whole class is moved by this war time scene.
At eighty-one I've learnt to surf the net.

It's taken nearly sixty years to let
me release these tears over what has been.
At eighty-one I've learnt to surf the net
found a haunting picture I can't forget.

Denise Bennett
England

Edelweiss

Often I find her alone in her room
staring into space; she has come upstairs to escape.
She cannot bear the bizarre behaviour
of some of the other residents –
those who constantly clamour to go home;
who lift their skirts at mealtimes,
filch her jewellery, hit her with handbags.

She has danced with her own demons,
wrestled with devils but they sit gentle now;
she received her medication like sacrament,
offers up her silence as prayer
but like the others, she is category G
kept behind locked doors.

The carers are kind but firm,
know nothing of her Devon childhood –
how she used to kick a pig's bladder
blown up for a football, with her brothers;
how she screamed when Harry put
a live bat down her back;
how she laughed when Bert tried out
one of the coffins in Jim Vane's shed;
how she clawed and spat at Miss Sear, the village
school teacher who singled out her sister
by her hair in front of the class.
They do not know the church linnet
who perched in the choir pew
for nine years,
do not brush her burnished copper curls.
They have never seen her in a charabanc,
simmering with excitement on a summer outing
wearing her new lavender dress –

and they do not know how she wept as a war widow
with a child of six weeks in her arms
when the sailor she loved was drowned.

She is blossom of snow now,
growing from the crevice of her chair –
small and white.
Sharon or Viv or Lisa dispense medicine
or food, help her bath. She is planning to run away
but they do not know.

Denise Bennett
England

To an Unpublished War Poet
(Flight Sergeant C. Mortimer 1916–98)

This poet was not a pacifist.
Enlisting before his call-up papers came,
he harnessed his love of engines to the war effort.

He never dropped a bomb or fired a gun,
but he bore the burden and the pain
of fixing aircraft engines,
flying with their test pilots,
and waiting in silence for his crews to return.

On the streets of Liverpool and Coventry
he saw what bombs can do;
a maternity hospital flattened,
new life crushed before it could even cry;
a cathedral reduced to a skeleton,
a charred cross held together by blackened nails.

This poet did not smile with his comrades
in the squadron photograph,
or raise a glass to victory on VE Day.
Back home with his family,
he could not bear to hear his newborn baby cry.

A man of few words
and no great literary aspirations,
in one private moment of righteous anger,
he sent back his medals
and penned a protest
that no one heard.

His words are buried
in some dusty, forgotten file,
never again to see the light of day,
like the people of Dresden,
wiped out in an act of vengeful retaliation,
when the war was already won.

This poet would not march on Remembrance Day,
choosing instead, the private marking
of German grief and graves he had never seen.

No history book records his protest.
No book of war poets publishes his name.
A man of few words
and no great literary aspirations,
yet a poet nonetheless.

I write these words to publish his protest,
to proclaim and honour his name.

Jean Mortimer
England

Wilson Carlile
(He Means Business)

A lifelong spinal problem proved no bar
to the Church Army's founder, Wilson Carlile.
During the Franco-Prussian war
his business prospered and in the meanwhile
he mastered German, French, Italian;
then came a slump, not in the business plan.

It ruined him, and brought an illness on.
Yet he was deputy-organist to Sankey
and Moody, we read next. Ordained a deacon,
curate in Kensington, folk thought him cranky,
and in the slums he often met with violence,
when into the world of altar-cloth and incense

he brought the evangelism of working men.
Grieved at the Church's gap of class, he sought
to bridge it, with each church a base camp; then
set out to see the needful training brought

within the reach of every 'Army mister';
later to women, through Maria, his sister.

Due in part to his humility, he gave
each Army worker much autonomy,
and saw to it that each of them should have
support with the responsibility.
Spent nights on the Embankment;* sat in cells;
established homes for tramps and ne'er-do-wells,

believing that the ne'er-do-well can do
as well as you or I if listened to.
His outdoor meetings caused such crowds and stew,
obstructing traffic, that he was asked to
stop holding them; the indoor halls he fills.
Like Christ's his work goes on, despite his ills.

Brian Louis Pearce
England

* London street alongside the River Thames

Pray for Me

One Sunday a young child was 'playing up' during morning
worship. The parents did their best to maintain some sort of
order in the pew but were losing the battle. Finally, the father
picked up the little fellow and walked sternly up the aisle on
his way out. Just before reaching the safety of the foyer, the little
one called out loudly to the congregation, 'Pray for me! Pray
for me!'

Anne Sardeson
England

Woman of Wisdom

Woman of wisdom, Spirit filled,
May we stand with you at the well.
May the new life you come to know
Rest upon all who seek to grow.

194

Woman of wisdom, without fear,
Reach out to touch the Saviour's hem.
Share with us healing you receive.
Show us anew we can believe.

Woman of wisdom, seeking yet
A place at table to be fed.
Claim your desire for spir'tual food.
We seek with you to be renewed.

Woman of wisdom, coins in hand,
Striving to follow faith's demand.
Generous widow, help us to give.
Through your example, may live.

Woman of wisdom at Christ's feet
Learning and sharing words of life.
Beside you there we find a space
To know the blessings of his grace.

Michael Jacob Kooiman
Canada

Lydia

Stubborn Huguenots
don't bow towards the Altar.
She stands there with her back to us,
like someone at a bus stop.
The liturgy flows from her
with authority and precision
but her sermon loses its nerve
and skitters about
gathering wool and a few gems.

She has bilingual genes.
At a NATO conference

she translates an American General
into English without knowing it.
The French Generals laugh
and say it was good,
but could she please
do it in French next time.

Having been a refugee
she goes out to scour the waysides
for Chileans and Vietnamese,
and fiercely mothers
a lovely Tutsi princess
against all menaces from
Hutu and Home Office.

Body and soul have asthma,
but she always has breath
for people on the edge of life.
She has been to the brink
and on just one occasion speaks
in a matter of fact way about
a glorious brightness.

It casts long shadows.
She tells me that one midnight
she thought she was going mad
and let herself into the church
to put her arms round a pillar.

Now I see her leaning forward,
large and serious. She says
she feels dead inside.
I hear it and lose the moment
somewhere inside my labyrinth.

Unheard, she drags herself *chez lui*
on the coach, too weak
to cope with airports,

and dies in downtown Paris
on the French NHS.

They bring her *home*
for her funeral, near the pillar.
I point it out, tell the story,
and this time I hear what she was saying.

Geoffrey Herbert
England

Known by Name

Who were you, Mary
From whom devils were cast out?
Did you disturb respectability
By washing his feet with tears.
An uninvited guest;
Or in embarrassing extravagance
Pour precious ointment on his head?
Were you notorious in your day,
Or a woman in the crowd from Magdala,
Who found her purpose
Being set free to love,
And used your gifts
In faithful ministry?

Perhaps it doesn't matter.
Perhaps, like all of us,
You were a mixture:
Damaged and healed;
Longing to be loved,
And struggling to relate;
Passionate and reserved
By turns, working out
Costly discipleship.

The important moment
Was when you heard your name,

197

And answered and were sent,.
No longer clinging to what kept you safe,
Strong in the power of the risen Lord,
To witness to new life.

Ann Lewin
England

To Katie*

She dared to climb the mountain,
Seeking accepting affinity.
It erupted,
Crashing,
Seeking to crush
Life,
Leaving her with
The awe-ful task
Of saving herself,
And others who came,
From the excruciating force,
The crescendoing fall
Of hot air and rock
Relying always, on God.

Claire Smith
Guyana

Blue Tulips
(on the engagement of Angela and Christine)

I plant the bulbs
which you gave me
in the Delft pot –
your present from Amsterdam;

* Dedicated to Revd Dr Katie Cannon, first African-American woman to
be ordained in the Presbyterian Church (USA)

covered with compost,
place the bowl in a cool, dark spot
and wait.

When they are well rooted
I bring them out
into a light, warm room.

In six weeks
they show signs of growth;
thin winter sun

forcing green shoots
from the secrecy of soil.
They rise, shining like

altar candles, blazing
cobalt flames, flowers unfurled
blue tulips
tender as your young love.

Elizabeth Cambridge
England

Them and Us
(A mother's meditation and prayer on homophobia)

These people are not like *us*.
We have nothing in common with *them*.
When *they* come out of the closet,
demand *their* rights,
organise *their* marches,
celebrate Gay Pride,
and tell *us* that *they're* glad to be Gay,
their candour disturbs *us*;
they make *us* squirm.
We wish *they* would go away.
We don't want *them* near *our* children.
They should stick together

199

with *their* own perverted kind.
They are sinful – cursed by infection.
Why should *we* pay taxes
to provide treatment and care
for *people like them?*
Let *them* pay the price of *their* evil ways.
We don't want *them* in *our* church.
How could God call *people like them*
to preach and minister to *people like us?*

These people live on *our* street,
sit beside *us* on the bus,
stand next to *us* in the checkout queue,
work alongside *us*,
cheer with *us* on the terraces,
and raise *their* glasses in *our* local wine bars and pubs.

These people have parents, partners and friends.
They laugh and cry and make love.
Though they cannot make children together,
each one is a child of God –
some mother's daughter or son,
and one of their number is mine.

Prayer
God, our Mother and Father,
Jesus, our Blood Brother,
Holy Spirit, our Loving Friend,
Remove the labels of us and them
that hang round our necks and keep us apart.
Break down the walls of fear and hatred.
Bind up the wounds of body, mind and heart.

Jean Mortimer
England

Nathanael

a man in whom there is no guile (John 1.47)

In a sunlit crescendo moment I glimpsed him
under the fig tree, and as he turns it's like seeing
right into his heart, seeing the bright iris
of longing, the place where there is no guile
to mask face from face.

We give one another the honour of seeing and listening.
We sit still because there's a lift of quiet hope
that at last our speech and our unspoken
will become understood, or, if not understood,
received and treasured.

So all pain and joy can be lit up,
and angels will ascend and descend
wherever God and humanity blend like this.

Geoffrey Herbert
England

The Glass in the Dustbin

Introduction

The glass ended up in the dustbin. It was my very first response
to a friend of mine, who contracted HIV. Instead of responding with love and solidarity, expressed in care and support I
avoided my brother-in-Christ for a couple of weeks.

Lord, Make Me Calm

On a warm summer's morning Steward stepped into our house.
We have been friends for more than 20 years. 'I have something important to share with you,' he said. 'I want to break
the silence. You are my friend and I trust you and have a deep
desire to share with you my concerns, fears and my emotions:

201

I am HIV positive', he said. 'I died two weeks ago when I was diagnosed.'

I felt like someone had just punched me in the stomach. I know I had to deal with HIV positive people, as a minister, in our community. But, my friend, not my friend. I managed to stay calm and did not do well with the rest of our conversation.

Then the absolute test. Steward poured himself a glass of water from the jug which was on the table in one corner. Minutes later my 30-month-old son walked into the room and took the glass from the tray. Scared that my son would drink the last drops of water from the glass, I ordered him in a very firm voice to leave the glass on the tray, and proceeded to literally pushed him out by the study door.

I immediately realized that this action of mine did more harm than good to our friendship. Through my action I contributed towards Steward's pain and suffering and the rest of his visitation did not last very long.

Steward left and the glass ended up in the dustbin.

Human Sinfulness

Steward left not only my study that morning he also left me with feelings, emotions and a challenge to embrace him for who he is. I avoided Steward for a couple of weeks and in the process contributed towards destroying and damaging his fragile human dignity.

Reflecting on my relationship with Steward I have come to the realisation that my friend challenged me to shift my understanding of acceptance. I have also come to the realisation that my actions were sinful and it was only through this acknowledgement of my human sinfulness, and the working of the Holy Spirit in my life that I have learned to love and care for my friend for who he is.

Through painful introspection I have learned we are not called simply to offer charity to a person who has AIDS but we must love them as we love ourselves. Romans 3.23 indicates that 'we all have sinned and fall short of the glory of God'. Recognition of our human sinfulness leads to spiritual growth.

From Diagnosis to Death

Steward was called to higher service at the age of 39. A small group of people were singing songs of praise at his bedside. I have journeyed alongside my friend from diagnosis to death and I am grateful. Three years before his death Steward left his employment and began to minister to communities in the rural areas of our country. Steward died, having a few clothes and a cellular phone as his only possessions.

Killed by the Stigma

AIDS is a very stigmatized issue. On one occasion Nelson Mandela uttered these words: 'Many who suffer from HIV and AIDS are not killed by the virus but by the stigma.' Society is prejudiced against AIDS patients and the stigma is exacerbated by fear. We are challenged to journey alongside those in our midst who suffer from HIV and AIDS from diagnosis to death.

Fragile Human Dignity

The Church is the body of Christ and a place where God's healing love is experienced and not a place where denigrating preaching of ministers damages and destroys the fragile human dignity of HIV and AIDS sufferers. Denigrating preaching results in the alienation of HIV and AIDS persons from the Church.

One of the wonderful characteristics of Jesus Christ is that he came so that those who are excluded are included. Jesus Christ came that the outsiders are no longer aliens. Instead of being hospitable the Church pushes many of God's children to the outskirts of Church and society.

No Barriers

Steward was a deeply committed Christian. He was my friend. Today he is free from all earthly pain and suffering.

I have learned that it is demanding to follow the way of Jesus in relationships. Jesus Christ acknowledged no barriers but always sought the well-being of all persons. Jesus showed in practice what it is to live in relationship with God.

Christ has challenged my relationship with Steward. I was called to extend my understanding.

Steward I salute you, may you rest in peace.

Steward was not my friend's real name

Kelvin Harris
South Africa

5

Proclaim Release for Prisoners

I was in prison and you visited me.
Matthew 25.36

The call today often embraces the great need to remember all the broken people of the world, especially people who are imprisoned by psychological walls . . . political walls . . . concrete walls . . . prejudicial walls.

There are women who live in the prison of a violent relationship, children who live in fear of the bully, and in the prison of abuse and abandonment, people who are living within a curfew. Heather Johnston's 'Bullying: A Victim's Prayer' (page **230**) which will resonate with many people both children and adults, 'The Concrete Wall' by Andrew Ashdown (page **221**) written after a visit to Palestine, and 'Reading Between the Lines' by Jean Mortimer (page **218**) all remind us of the importance of releasing women, men and children from their various prisons.

I Believe . . .

I believe in the sun, even when it is not shining.
I believe in love, even when I don't feel it.
I believe in God, even when he doesn't answer.

The Warsaw Ghetto
Poland

Welcome, Mordechai

His crime was alerting the world
to a nuclear threat.
His warnings were for the welfare
of his own and other countries.
This is the true patriotism
of a global citizen.
He was accused by State leaders
who themselves had a case to answer
for crimes against humanity.
He was found guilty
by a legal system with a clear bias.
He endured years of imprisonment,
including many in solitary confinement.
His punishment went far beyond
a reasoned response to whistle-blowing.
His commitment did not lessen;
his spirit was not broken.
The day of his release, even then conditional,
was greeted with global acclamation.
His concern for the world is recognised
and his compassion is applauded.
Welcome, Mordechai.

John Johansen-Berg
England

The Prisoner

Remember me?
I'm the prisoner sent down
for crimes against
Humanity.
Who yearns
to be set free
from my guilt and grief
and depravity.

To be at peace
With those I've wounded.

To know
the healing balm
of their forgiveness.

The calm
still waters
of that healing well.

Jesus,
Turn this stagnant water
that is me,
into the New Wine
that is of you.

And,
my fellow human traveller,
what of *you*?
What are *your* crimes
against Humanity?

What need
have you left undone,
turned from,
or walked by on the other side?

Are you just as much
a prisoner
as me?

Are you held captive
by your indifference?

Susan Hardwick
England

Release

The blindfold is removed.
Joy to see again,
delight in the dazzling,
colour, movement, distance.
Lord, how wonderful
that I can use my eyes and see your world.

The gag is removed.
For so long I have been dumb,
not one critical word,
not one cry for help.
But now I am free to speak
And declare my truth.
Lord, how wonderful
that you are the Word
and we too can speak openly.

The leg-irons are removed.
So tightly confined,
the pressure sores got worse
and the muscles weak.
But now, I can walk, jump, run.
I can move across your world.
Lord, how wonderful
is this freedom of movement.

The handcuffs are removed.
It is the hardest thing,
not being able to touch you;
never feeling a cat's fur
or the wood's grain
or the marble's chill.
Lord, wonderful is your touch,
your touch on my life,
and today embracing friends.

Bernard Thorogood
Australia

Let's Call Her Jackie

She under-achieved at school except when on the stage.
She felt her teachers belonged to a drab and distant age.
She was eager and lively, wanted to do things 'for kicks'.
She joined a gang of youngsters who knew all sorts of tricks –
How to steal in supermarkets, to force open expensive cars,
how to get alcohol under age in certain shops and bars.
One night she joined an affray after excessive drinking:
Her actions were extremely wild – she was past the stage of
    thinking.

Jackie is in the girls' wing of a sombre adult prison.
At meal-times with adult inmates there is no clear division.
Jackie misses McDonald's and going about in a gang
discussing football and pop stars and the latest teenage
    slang.
Sometimes she listens to the radio while 'banged up' in a
    cell.
She longs for more 'with it' clothing, pretty underwear as
    well.
She seldom gets a letter from a friend or her troubled
    mother –
a hard-pressed single parent who dotes on her little brother.

Positive steps are now being taken to improve Jackie's education and she is beginning to overcome her loneliness and frustration. A prison visitor recommended a sensible, practical way of training her for employment which ensures at least reasonable pay. She dreaded her eighteenth birthday in case everyone would forget. A few cards came – one from an aunt she'd never actually met. The letter from her mother told of her aches and pains and fatigue but Jackie got her new tracksuit bottoms – a gift from the Howard League.*

Rosemary Watts
England

The Kingdom Has Come Close
(Mark 1.15)

The night is a prison for glory.
I shall cleave it open with God's lightning and let you out,
all you jailbirds of the dark, and we'll fly.

The sparrows know about this, and the children,
it's hidden in the heart of mustard seeds and desert flowers,
the springs and vines and harvests,
in everything living on the brink of hope.
It's the cup we shall drink together
and the bread we shall hand each other.

The shadows know about it too,
edge to edge with us like swords.
You and I will fight them
and we can win.

Geoffrey Herbert
England

* The Howard League for Penal Reform aids girls in prison by listening to their problems, helping to find suitable courses and making gifts where appropriate.

In Their World

'Time is important,'
They say.
It is their world.

'People are important,'
We say
In our world.

It is their world
We struggle in,
Making it,
Not,
Seeking only to survive,

In their world.

Claire Smith
Guyana

Release of Prisoners

Then was a time of darkness,
confined in damp and dirty rooms,
imprisoned by walls and bars;
no window to see the sky
or to hear the birds' song at dawn.
Then there was the torture of physical beatings,
the terror of mental stress, the nights of spiritual testing.
Now is a time of liberation.
People did not forget; they spoke; they acted.
So the prison doors are opened;
the prisoner sees again God's sky,
hears the myriad sounds of nature
and is welcomed with open arms.
The days of testing are over;
the spirit rejoices in God our Saviour.

John Johansen-Berg
England

The Silent Prisoner

Visiting hour comes around
with regularity
and names are called
and favoured ones
emerge from cells
to see some loved one
through another cell
glass-walled
while others wait
in silence –
their names not called.
But God sends messengers
beyond the bars
to cheer the silent ones
to throw a rope of hope
to those whose dreams
are lost among the stars.

Harry Wiggett
South Africa

1.30pm HMP Holloway

All pushing baby-buggies
And wearing their sunglasses,
Security-cleared passes,
The officers will come.

From Holloway, from prison,
When dinner-time is over,
Out through a sliding doorway
The lines of pushchairs come.

They're taking out the babies,
The inmates' tiny babies,
The brown and pinkish babies
Of the imprisoned mums.

213

They're taking out the babies
To glimpse some other places,
To get air on their faces.
Not prisoners like their mums.

The line of pushchairs passes
A line of older children
And toddlers with their Aunties,
Queuing to see their mums.

The guard behind the glass is
Examining the passes
And scrutinizing faces
Before they meet their mums.

Lucy Berry
England

The Public Has Forgotten Them

Condemned by the media, hated for a spell
but forgotten now in prison-workroom or cell,
the women-lifers spend their troubled days
out of our sight – out of the public gaze.
Few think about their loneliness or tears.
Few can understand their anxieties and fears.
Some women fear loss of fertility before release.
The middle-aged dread close relatives' decease
before they once again can live as those outside.
Some harm themselves and only want to hide.
Some are keen to work towards their reformation
but dread the required changes of prison location.
Some lack the kind of clothes that would restore some pride.
Some would like more courses than the system can provide.
All gladly receive letters and telephone communication,
All need our prayers for their health and restoration.

Rosemary Watts
England

I Flew

He said,
'Come to the edge.'
I said,
'I can't, I'm afraid.'
He said,
'Come to the edge,'
I said,
'I can't, I'll fall off.'
He said, finally,
'Come to the edge.'
And I came to the edge,
And
       I flew.

Guillaume Apollinaire
(1880–1918)

We Come Together in Freedom

As we come together today in freedom, we pray for all those who are imprisoned. For men and women beating their heads against prison walls. For butterflies beating their wings against panes of glass. For animals pacing up and down in cages. For all people caged by poverty, addictions, oppression, violence, fear or guilt.

Grant them and us the freedom of spirit that never gives up hope and which in Christ never dies.
Amen.

Lynne Chitty
England

A Kiss in Waitrose

My wife is not often surprised by what happens but when a woman on the other end of an aisle in Waitrose* suddenly squealed my name and rushed up to us and grabbed me in an affectionate hug and kissed me, I could see that she was struggling to think what to do and what had led to this unusual occurrence. Kelly didn't stay long but did briefly explain to Janet that I had saved her life some ten years ago by giving her such wonderful support and encouragement when she had been at the point of killing herself because life had become so awful. Now she was free from her brutal husband, her children were grown up and she was now running a shelter for women who had suffered as she had done. Then she was gone, thanking me as she went and blowing a final kiss down the aisle.

I did remember her and she was indeed a changed person. When I had known her she was on her own with two young children in very substandard accommodation. Her husband had recently gone to prison leaving her with massive debts. His treatment of her had resulted in the loss of any friends and most of her family. She had been truly alone and in desperate circumstances. Although I helped by getting her some early financial support and some new furniture to replace the goods taken by the bailiffs, most of what I did was to support her in going to the right places to sort out for herself what needed to be done. It was a long and slow process, not helped when she lost her baby by miscarriage and suffered a depressive breakdown. She was only on probation for a year but I continued to see her for about six months just to make sure she was able to cope. When she was moved to decent accommodation I lost contact until that kiss!

Colin Ferguson
England

* a supermarket in the United Kingdom

In Equal Measure

One red shirt
hung on washing line
makes me stop and stare.
Some days I see the sadness
of Christ suffering
almost everywhere.

But then

Folding it later;
faint scent of damask rose,
sweet evening air,
the evidence of Christ
living, I'm uplifted
into joyful prayer.

Eve Jackson
England

The Invader

You invade our world
You turn it upside down;
Despoil our Land
Kill the innocent,
And then you turn
And call us stupid.

You depopulate our lands
Break up our communities;
Destroy our leaders
Leave us gutted,
And then you turn
And call us aimless.

217

You bring us to your world
Take away our selfhood;
Rob us of our being
Label us subhuman,
And then you turn
And call us shiftless.

You impose your values
Push ours out the door;
Commoditize life
Scoff when we celebrate life,
And then you turn
And call us losers.

And we all cry freedom,
We all cry equality,
We all cry God
Of Justice, hear us.

Claire Smith
Guyana

Reading Between the Lines
*(A meditation on slavery, ancient and modern,
based on Genesis 16; Genesis 21.1–21; Galatians 4.21–31)*

I know about slavery.
Its scars mark my body.
They are branded on my heart.

The scars of separation
from family and homeland,
security and love;

The scars of rape;
lost innocence and trust,
stolen by a master

218

who used me
to get himself a son,
ignored me and cast me aside;

The scars of abuse
and abandonment;
harsh words of hatred,
spat in my face,
and hurled at my fleeing back,
by a scornful mistress,
jealous of me and my son;

The scars of hunger and thirst;
alone in a hostile wilderness,
not knowing how to keep
my son and myself alive,
or bear the anguish
of watching him die.

God knows about slavery.
Its scars mark other bodies.
They are branded on many hearts.

Don't claim that you do not know me.
Don't turn a deaf ear to my cries.
I AM HAGAR. GOD HAS SEEN ME.
I HAVE NAMED GOD. I HAVE SURVIVED.

Don't rape me with smart rhetoric,
or allegorise me away.
HEAR MY STORIES. READ THEM AND WEEP
FOR HAGAR AND ISHMAEL TODAY.

Jean Mortimer
England

The Passion of the Christ

Jesus suffered,
it pulled no punches, the film was clear.
Jesus suffered,
there was hatred and fear.
There was blood
the skin was torn.
Jesus was good
the audience worn.

Evil everywhere, cloaked in religious garb.

Jesus suffered,
the film was clear!

Was this that moved you, all powerful God, finally to
    forgive?

That film,
brings home the horror of torture, today.
The plight of prisoner, of conscience, of whatever
beaten, abused, dehumanised.

The Passion of the Christ?
A film for all prisoners,
for all victims of torture
for every person abused.
It is going on, and worse . . .

Holy, Compassionate, Just God
You're waiting for me to speak for the victims
in prison, in homes, in isolated despair and pain.

Forgive me, if ignoring them, I hold it all for *my* gain!

John Ll. Humphreys
Scotland/Wales

The Other End of the Street

If I go up
to the other end
of my street,
I can choose
left or right,
go where I will
go when I will.

They can't go up
to the other end
of their street
they can't choose
left or right
go where they will
go when they will

It's different in Palestine
curfew,
guns,
and tanks.

Patricia Price-Tomes
Israel/Palestine/England

The Concrete Wall

'We will cut off your electricity and your water supplies. You
will be like a dead olive tree.' With these words a few months
ago, the soldiers left the house of an elderly Palestinian woman in a small village east of Bethlehem. They had asked her
and her family to leave the home and the land that the family
have nurtured for nearly 200 years. In the valley, the ancient
olive groves, comprising of trees that were originally planted
by the Romans, have been completely uprooted to make

221

way for the eight-metre high concrete wall that now snakes for hundreds of kilometres around the Palestinian territories destroying thousands of acres of land and hundreds of homes – everything in its wake, cutting people off from families, work, schools, clinics, shops. Across the valley yet another new settlement is being built on land that the farmers have cultivated for centuries. When the wall is complete, the villagers will not have access to the nearest school or clinic. And checkpoints the other side of the village will in effect imprison them in their own homes. Without electricity or water the villagers will almost certainly be forced out. This is the reality for dozens of ancient Palestinian communities today. Human rights abuses being committed daily on a vast scale against a whole civilian population entirely against international law. Yet the world not only remains silent, but politically, militarily and financially supports the injustices of the aggressor.

Andrew Ashdown
England

Yo creo en Nicaragua
(I Believe in Nicaragua)

1. In the eyes of a child waiting for hope to come
   In the eyes of a child of Nicaragua
   You see the pain of today as the world looks away
   From the streets and the fields of Nicaragua

Chorus:
Yo creo en Nicaragua
Yo creo en los niños
Creo en el mañana
Yo creo en Nicaragua

2. There was a time that gave a voice to those who had
   never spoken
   There was a time of fresh hope in Nicaragua

But once again they've been silenced by the powerful
   from the north
And their friends in high places of corruption

Chorus:
Yo creo en Nicaragua . . .

3.   The sweatshops have arrived – the only way to survive
        And so people become slaves once again
        Not allowed to have a union, not allowed to have a voice
        In this globalisation game they have no choice

Chorus
Yo creo en Nicaragua . . .

Garth Hewitt
England

The Prison of Prejudice

Steel doors and iron bars are not the only prisons.
Cruel words and harsh actions,
cultural demands and ancient prejudices,
the taunts of children and innuendoes from neighbours,
all make a kind of prison.
From some prisons there is early release
as a reward for good conduct.
In the harsh prison of communal condemnation
there is no hope of release,
but a long prospect of cruelty
that brings despair and desperation.

John Johansen-Berg
England

A Prayer for Prison Chaplains

Jesus,
you proclaimed that you had come
to set the prisoner free.

We think of the very special work
of Prison Chaplains.
Walk with them.
Guide them and
give them the wisdom
and the strength they need
to do the daily task.

Give them compassion
and imagination
and a ready sense of humour,
for all the situations
within which they work.
May they be your face
to all whom they meet.

May they always be blessed
with the knowledge
even on the most difficult of days –
that those in their care
bear the imprint of Christ
upon their souls.

Help them to treat all
with whom they work
with respect and dignity,
just as you would have done.

Susan Hardwick
England

The Shadow in the Middle

Serving Lord, it is too easy to be the shadow in the middle
pointing the finger of blame – quick to condemn and slow to
forgive.

You hesitated – you did not respond quickly – your gut
instinct was not to condemn but to restore.

May we see through the eyes of others – and listen and
understand and recognise how we would have behaved in
similar circumstances and under similar pressures.

As we seek to be those living right may we never fail to
empathise, to understand, to forgive and where possible
to restore

because this is what you have done to us and continue to do
for us.

Your grace and mercy is our hope – may we pass it on to
others so that the bitter seed of self-righteousness is not
allowed to grow in us.

and to continue with the song

1.   I see him in a prison cell, they say he deserves to die
        They see her on the street – 'we've caught her', they cry
        We all call out 'guilty', and fingers point in blame
        But you're writing in the dust and you turn your face
        away.

2.   I see him so desperate, driven to despair
        No-one would listen, so he took the road to terror
        We all know he's guilty, and cry 'vengeance shall have its
        day'

But you're writing in the dust and you turn your face
away.

Chorus:
Who is the shadow in the middle?
Who will be the first to lay the blame?
You turn and look at the shadow in the middle
I see the shadow in the middle bears my name.

3. We always know the guilty ones, we're so quick to
criticise
But who is quick to listen, and to ask the question
'why?'
Looking through another's eyes, I remember what you'd
say
As you're writing in the dust, and you turn your face
away.

Chorus:
Who is the shadow in the middle . . .

4. Are you writing in the dust to get your thinking clear?
To give yourself some time, to listen and to hear?
Can we find a way to live that cares and listens more?
Can we take the same path as you would do, Lord?

Chorus:
Who is the shadow in the middle . . .

Garth Hewitt
England

Potatoes

Ken was released from Borstal early because they could not control him. He had a string of violent offences behind him and he had already told the Borstal welfare officer what he could do with the licence I had to supervise. I was therefore slightly surprised when he reported. I decided that I would accept his opinion about licence and so I laid down the minimum that he had to conform to and promised that I would not expect any more than that unless he asked me. I then said, and why I did I cannot remember, 'But if I were you, I would want to know how I can turn all that anger into something positive so that it helps me rather than hurting others and destroying my life.' He looked at me as if I was crazy but he asked the question, 'What do you mean?'

Over the next few months Ken's life began to stabilise. He found a job that used up a lot of his energy in a greengrocers and he joined a local rugby team. That didn't last very long but at least it gave him the idea that the anger burning inside him might have a way of being safely contained. By being able to talk about his anger and to share the violence and abuse he had suffered as a child without being judged or threatened with punishment for what was ingrained in him, he slowly began to feel in control of his life. When he found Heather it was like he had suddenly been forgiven. Life had meaning.

Ken kept in touch with me after his licence finished. He became manager of the shop and his boss effectively treated him as his own son. The anger was still there and did flare up from time to time, but now that he was aware of it and how it could affect him, he had developed his own little strategies for dealing with it. In the last letter I received from Ken he added a postscript, 'P.S. When it gets too much for me now, I take it out on the potatoes, love, Ken.' Too often we are scared away by people's anger, failing to see the hurt person inside the violence. By recognising him as someone who could accept that anger and use it, instead of denying it and punishing him

for it, Ken became a hard-working, loving father and husband
even though he still needed the potatoes.

Colin Ferguson
England

Honour or Liberty

Tradition says she must marry this man
though her heart tells her that she loves another.
Her culture and religion give her father authority
so she is expected to bow gracefully to the inevitable.
Yet the freedom she sees in a new land
questions the culture of the old country.
She is pulled this way and that
and can see no way out of the conflict.
Where can she turn?
She looks at the handful of tablets
and asks, 'Is this my liberation?'
She is faced with a grim dilemma.
Is it not possible to honour her father
yet not betray her true love?

John Johansen-Berg
England

I Walk in Liberty

When the wind blows
the wind is in my voice

When the rain falls hard
the rain is in my pain

When the sun shines
the sun is in my smile

When the animals run through the meadows
I walk in liberty

When you cry
I hear your cry for help

When you smile
the world and I
smile.

Zola F.
England

Playtime of Terror

Day after day he endures the mockery,
term after term he suffers the blows,
a victim of the combined power of the bullies.
Occasionally another boy
gives whispered words of encouragement,
yet not too openly lest he too becomes a victim.
How long can this go on?
His endurance is tested week after week
of silent agony and suffering.
He stares at the loop of rope
and looks up at the rafter.
There seems no other way to be free
unless some stranger cares enough to intervene
and offer a better way of liberation.

John Johansen-Berg
England

Bullying: A Victim's Prayer

Lord, I'm being bullied
I don't know what to do.
Should I tell
and risk more bullying?
Or turn the other cheek
and put up with it?

Lord, what would you do
if you were being bullied today?
You were bullied
by the Pharisees and leaders.
You didn't give in,
you stood up to their questions –

until the end came.
But you knew that was your destiny,
you had to make the ultimate sacrifice,
you had to obey.
Yet you understood
and you forgave them.

Lord, please give me
the courage to stand up to them with the right words;
the wisdom to know when to keep silent;
the insight to understand them,
the love to forgive them –

and the determination not to be a bully myself.

Amen

Heather Johnston
Scotland

Preaching to the Confused

Songs of Praise in the day room of a psycho-geriatric ward

> They are not here by choice
> But one picks up a once familiar tune
> And, rocking to and fro begins to croon
>   In quavering voice.
>
> They are not here to praise
> But, wheeled or wandering in, consent to stay
> If only as a not unpleasant way
>   To pass their days.
>
> They are not here to pray
> But by this service, Lord, may I impart
> Some thought or hope of peace to one sad heart
>   For you, today.

Barbara Moss
England

Our Hospital, Our Garden

The Gardeners' Department was situated in a small brick quadrangle, near to the Vegetable Preparation room. Most of the time, of course, the gardeners were somewhere around about the grounds, mowing the lawns, weeding the huge flower beds, sweeping up leaves, rolling the playing fields. There always seemed to be a lot of them and it was impossible to tell who was an employee from outside the hospital and who a patient whose home was here, on one of the long-stay wards. The gardeners were very proud of their handiwork and would pause and share their pleasure with anyone with a moment to spare. They had every reason to feel proud; in summer their flowers surrounded the hospital with a penumbra of colour, like a dark stone in a summer garden. When it was really hot the staff brought elderly men and women in geriatric chairs down in the lift and wheeled them onto the lawn where, among the flower beds, the emotional casualties of twentieth-century living lay on the grass in their swimming costumes, sunbathing.

When autumn came the gardeners loaded a wagon with flowers and vegetables and fastened it to the rear of the tractor to transport it along the gravel road to the hospital church for the Harvest Festival. This wide swathe of urban countryside belonged to the hospital patients. The space was not simply to separate two worlds but to give patients the chance to rest for a little between worlds. At Easter, the church was usually full of flowers and stood in the middle of a host of daffodils. On one occasion, however, the gardeners had forgotten and the congregation arrived to an empty church. Before the service began, one of the patients rushed in, her arms bursting with daffodils which she had obviously gathered from the ones around the church. 'After all', she said, 'it's our garden, isn't it?'

Roger Grainger
England

Butterfly Child

Helpless you lie, Butterfly Child,
pinned on a cork, wings open, shame.
Private display stimulates him;
sick dread as he stabs you again.

Broken you lie, Butterfly Girl,
held on the mattress, legs open wide.
'Get pregnant and you're dead' is the threat,
as he mounts for his latest ride.

Bleeding you lie, Butterfly Mine,
curled on the bed, nursing our wounds.
Break the silence of many years.
Let the truth flood into this room.

Anon

232

A Litany of Blessing and Anointing
(for those who have been sexually abused)

For three friends whose courage has touched my heart and given me these words.

>Loving, Protecting, Nurturing One,
>our creator and carer,
>Obedient, Suffering, Self-Giving Son,
>our friend and brother,
>Enabling, Guiding, Strengthening Spirit,
>our companion and sister,
>Uniquely separate,
>Uniquely whole;
>Trinity in unity,
>God in threefold nature and name;
>
>Be present with ....
>your wounded child.
>
>Come in love and protection
>to cradle her/him in your arms.
>
>Come in love and compassion
>to heal her/his brokenness
>with your gentle touch.
>
>Come in love and strength
>to help her/him to name her/his wounds.

The Touching and Anointing

(A bowl of fragrant oil may be used by both minister and participant to anoint each part of her/his body as it is named. If either is not comfortable with self-anointing this may be omitted.)

Wounded Person
I touch my throat (and anoint it)
that I may not be ashamed
to speak of my pain;
that my unspoken fears
may find a voice.

Minister
I touch my throat (and anoint it)
that I may speak of God's acceptance and love.

Wounded Person
I touch my ears (and anoint them)
that I may shut out the false, persuasive or threatening
    words
that told me ' never to tell ',
that I may hear new and enabling words of hope.

Minister
I touch my ears (and anoint them)
that I may listen attentively
and with sensitivity
to words that are painful to speak and to hear.

Wounded Person
I touch my eyelids (and anoint them)
for they have been closed too long,
to shut out the nightmare of my abuse,
that I may look upon the face of my oppressor
and see that it was his/her fault, not mine.

Minister
I touch my eyelids (and anoint them)
that my eyes, and the eyes of the world,
may never be closed with embarrassment or apathy,
that they may look with compassion upon
the eyes which register such pain.

Wounded Person
I touch my nose (and anoint it)
to rid my nostrils and my memory
of the smell of his/her body
upon mine.

Minister
I touch my nose (and anoint it)
that the fragrance of this aromatic oil
may fill our senses and help us
to feel the freshness of God's renewing love.

Wounded Person
I touch my lips (and anoint them)
that the sourness and staleness
of all my suffering may be sweetened
by the knowledge that God is good.

Minister
I touch my lips (and anoint them)
'O taste and see, that the Lord is good.
Blessed are you when you can place your
trust in God.'

Wounded Person
I touch my hands (and anoint them).
I let go of the images of powerful,
controlling hands, holding me down,
of my own weak and trembling hands,
helplessly flailing,
covering my face,
praying for rescue that never came.
I open my hands to receive and welcome
the gift of God's strength and love.

Minister
I touch my hands (and anoint them)
that I may dare to reach out
and feel my sister's/brother's pain.

Wounded Person
I touch my arms (and anoint them)
that they may cease to hold on to my hurt,
hugging it to myself;
that I may be open
to embrace new possibilities;
to trust myself to new encounters,
to reach out to others and to God.

Minister
I touch my arms (and anoint them)
that I may embrace my sister/brother,
enfold her/him in God's protective love
and support her/him in prayer.

Wounded Person
I touch my legs and feet (and anoint them)
that I may stand upright and tall,
walk with dignity and pride,
acknowledging the pain of the past,
instead of trying to run away,
and beginning a new journey
to self-discovery and self-respect.

Minister
I touch my legs and feet (and anoint them)
that I may stand alongside my sister/brother
in solidarity and strength;
that I may stand up and be counted
with all who oppose abuse
and seek to help the abused
and the abusers.

Wounded Person
I touch my head and my heart (and anoint them)
that my thoughts and feelings may be one;
that my heart will believe

what my head tells me is true;
that all painful or self-destructive thoughts
and feelings may be named and healed.

Minister
I touch my head and my heart (and anoint them)
that I may take time and trouble
to be more informed;
that I may ensure the protection
of every child in the church;
that I may demonstrate God's affirming love
in word and in deed.

Wounded Person
In this touching (and anointing)
of my body,
may I be healed and made whole.

Minister
In this touching (and anointing)
may the body of Christ,
broken for you and for me
be re-membered.

Amen

(Where it seems helpful and appropriate the minister may
invite the wounded person to touch or anoint more intimate
parts of her/his body when she/he is alone. The litany may
be followed by the sharing of bread and wine. It is advisable
to ensure that another person known and trusted by the
wounded person and the minister should be present when
this litany is said.)

Jean Mortimer
England

Three Mothers for Peace

She was a Jewish mother
who lost her daughter,
killed by a suicide bomber.
She did not therefore regard Palestinians
as enemies.
For her the real enemies are those
who use the violence of war as an instrument,
a means to gain supremacy and power.

This one was a Palestinian mother
Who lost her son,
killed by an Israeli military bullet.
Her son was not holding a gun,
not even a stone to throw at the tanks,
but the baby of a relative.
She did not call for revenge
but for peace and justice in both communities.

This one was a British woman
who chose to have her child
in the Palestinian maternity ward,
A baby born in Bethlehem.
She knew that some Arab women
never made it to the hospital,
detained at checkpoints, some to become fatalities.
She too longs for a just peace.

John Johansen-Berg
England

Mary's Psalm

There is no one to blame
for the death of my son –
and millennia of misery.

There is no one to censure
for a mother's torment –
and perennial seasons of evil.

There is no one to condemn
for your life or mine –
and the inhumanity of history.

There is no one to reproach
for inventories of horror
which abolish feelings.

There is no one to accuse
when women bring children
to watch a king killed –

When anemones
are stamped underfoot
in a reflex of indifference.

Why?

Derek Webster
England

Bella

Bella told our fortune in the tea cups,
taught in the Sunday School and served the meals
on weekdays. Bouquets made from buttercups
and daisies helped to make young bruises heal,
dried tears, brought smiles and made her young friends feel
that life was kind. In war few words were said;
her grief was quiet when her man was dead.
She soldiered on and never showed her cares
and we became the child she loved instead
of that which she had once hoped would be theirs.

Colin Ferguson
England

Survivor

She's my generation
a mother like me –
this quiet woman
modest in headscarf, grey dress –

my generation – standing here
barred from her family home
inside the fence. You could say
she's a lucky one
alive
outside the fence
presumed sane
and after all she has a son.

We were children, she and I
that year of our Lord
nineteen hundred and forty-eight.

There the likeness ends

That year she lost
home mother father uncles aunts
cousins grandparents 35 family members
not to mention neighbours and friends;
jumped through a window two floors up
and walked 5 kilometres to Jerusalem

I think I could give the rest of my life
feeling for empathy with
the emotions the memories the anguish
behind that quiet face, those tear-filled eyes

it's little short of miraculous
her presence, her sharing
outside the fence

Patricia Price-Tomes
Israel/Palestine/England

240

Friend Betsy
(Elizabeth Fry)

Of mercy, not of judgement,
she spoke to those she met;
in hope to show the women
that theirs were lives that yet,
though behind bars, could flower.

She did not hesitate
to go amongst the worst,
perceiving that she and
her like were but the first
of the condemned to flower

in Christ, who spoke within
her heart, and honoured her
straight answer: gave her strength
to go, Good Book in her
hand, to bid darkness flower.

Like Joshua's three hundred
were women she found crowded
into Newgate. Overnight
she blew a trump and lorded
the inner light she saw a flower

in them. She lifted them
up into heaven to
take tea with angels. Doing
the same for vagrants, too,
she gave them beds, a flower

of real love from her heart.
A long with others, relieved
the lot of convicts bound

for New South Wales; believed
we are here thus to flower.

Brian Louis Pearce
England

Human

Why should I bow my head
Why should I lower my eyes
Why should I not speak
Why should I sit inside
I am a living being like you
I want to lift up my head and walk
I want to look in life's eyes
I want to break the word to you:
I want to find a new path.

Sr Nasreen Daniel
Pakistan

Superwoman
Proverbs 31.10–31

Where do you find a good wife?
They're like gold-dust.

Of course, she must be able to have kids.
And be trustworthy.
And have her husband's interests at heart
Every day of her life.
And be able to make the clothes.

She'll drive miles to the shops to get the food in.
She'll get up at the crack of dawn
To cook the evening meal.

She's fair with the au pair.

She invests her earnings sensibly
In wines and spirits.
She's a determined, hard-working woman,
Burning the midnight oil, doing the accounts.

She does lovely crochet.

She's kind and practical with
People less fortunate than herself.

If it's nippy outside, don't worry;
She's already got out the winter clothes.

She knits her own bed covers.
She makes fetching garments out of linen –
And smart purple outfits.
Naturally, her husband is
Well-known and influential.

She has a business manufacturing retail-wear.
She's tough and has integrity
And she doesn't have to worry about tomorrow.
What she says is worth hearing.
She makes sense.

She keeps an eye on the au pair.
She never rests.

All her sons think she's great
And her husband is always saying
How marvellous she is:
'There are plenty of clever women out there,
But you put them all in the shade!'

A woman doesn't need to be charming or beautiful,
As long as she goes to church
And is well-respected.

Congratulations.
She should be famous.

Lucy Berry
England

6

The Despised and Rejected

Truly I tell you, just as you did it to one of the least of these
who are members of my family, you did it to me.

Matthew 25.40

People who are despised, rejected and cast off as no-good by
society are living, breathing human beings with emotions, who
suffer hurt in the same way as any other member of society.
These women and men of all ages need to be held safe in love
. . . the love of humankind . . . the love of God.

Father Padraig Regan has written 'A Saint of the Streets'
(page **200**) from his experiences of working with homeless
people; Claire Smith from Guyana expresses that 'Christ waits'
in 'The Least of These', (page **247**); and Wendy Whitehead
wishes everyone to 'Stretch out Your Hand' (page **254**) There
is a place in God's love for the people who are written about
in 'Minister Reaches Out' (page **270**) Compassion and help are
needed for women despised, as in 'Migrant' by Salvador T.
Martinez of Thailand (page **271**). People who live with leprosy
are remembered in 'Together We're Stronger', a story from The
Leprosy Mission (page **261**).

All food for thought and action.

Hold Us Safe in Your Love

You call by name every person on earth
and all belong to you.
Still our hearts that
we may know your compassion.
Hold us safe in your love and
help us to trust that those who die forgotten
by the world are not forgotten
in your sight and care.
You know them more profoundly than
we knew them and they belong to you.

*(Where you know a person who has died by living homeless on
the streets, an act of aggression such as homophobia or any other
unnatural cause please mention them here by name.)*

Please remember ....

Symbolising all in our care who died during this past year.

Roger Shaljean
England

The Least of These

They passed her by;
It seemed best.
She was only a drunk,
Unknown to them.
She'll sleep it off
At the roadside.
No need to soil
Their 'Sunday-best'.
She died,
As they prayed and sang
For the least of these.

Everyone stared,
As he walked up the aisle,
Quite unkempt,
With a sad smile.
He walked right up,
Sat on the floor.
What should they do?
The preacher walked down
Sat on the floor,
As they prayed and sang
For the least of these.

We pass them by
Everyday, everywhere,
But the least in us
Keeps us trapped in fear
Of seeming to be
The least of all;
Yet we sing and we pray
For the least of these.

And Christ waits.

Claire Smith
Guyana

Street Nightingales

(For young people who leave home and become homeless)

I have heard their harsh melodies
at the closing of the day,
brittle-voiced vespers
croaked to the death rattle
of empty-bellied beer cans
clanking in the gutter.

I have felt their wakeful numbness
on the South Bank walk-a-way;

cardboard clad jesters
cloaked in the drab grey dress
of Oxfam's picked over
and rejected clutter.

I have seen their vacant faces,
no place for a smile to stay;
silent protestors
choked in this city
of gala night gadabouts,
all done up in glitter.

Stillborn from death, aborted birds,
whose life Keats could not convey
with sad metaphors,
soaked in dull self-pity.
Swansong for street nightingales,
binned with London's litter.

Jean Mortimer
England

A Woman of the Streets

A woman of the streets
Is what is me
Not quite of life
But lifelike in my lifelessness
And faithful to the faceless fears
That follow me as friends might once
Have dared to do.
Unchanging are the sterile steps
That wear the pavement's patience
Day and night,
Night and day
Familiar feet

Pacing out their patterns
Day and night
Night and day.

My rancid rags would leave
But weighted down by wretchedness
And clad in concrete's dust and dirt
They trundle on
Their fate secured
Signed and sealed as mine
In fettered filth
Unlockable
Except perhaps by sweeper's brush.

A bundle in a doorway
Clothed in only
Yesterday
And what was me
Before the woman of the streets
Alive
At last.

Lynne Chitty
England

A Saint of the Streets

(A Reflection given at the Service of Commemoration for Homeless People who died on the streets of London UK in the previous year)

'God so loved the world that he gave his only Son so that whoever believes in him should have everlasting life' (John 3.16). I think of it as the most wonderful human statement or promise that has ever been uttered. It continues, completes and perfects the promise of Psalm 103.6, 'The Lord executes justice for all who are oppressed.'

Jack (Jake) Hill was known to many inhabitants of London's streets, as well as to many day centres. Jake died from an overdose of crack-cocaine. He was with two friends. His funeral was a loving farewell, dignified by the attendance of his two brothers. Jake was a man of just fifty summers. He was wilful but he was also wonderful. His large and generous humanity remained unimpaired. He was a deeply spiritual and a holy man.

Jake struggled with his addiction to alcohol and drugs. It may be said that the addiction killed him. News of his death occasioned a great outpouring of grief among his friends. People told stories as they remembered his life. 'He was my father.' 'Jake saved my life.'

He lived with hope in Jesus, the Son of God sent to bring salvation and hope. He once said to me, with that grim intensity with which he sometimes spiced his words, 'No matter how bad things are I have Jesus, he is my Saviour.'

'God so loved the world that he gave his only Son . . .'

Jake lived and died with that hope in his heart. A sinner much loved by Jesus Christ.

Jake was a saint of the streets.

Fr Padraig Regan
England/Ireland

have you ever?

have you ever lived in a house with no heat
and worn hand-me-down clothes?
have you ever cried at night
because you're completely alone?
have you ever NOT had your cake and eaten it too?

have you ever been an 'illegal' in a foreign land,
have you ever had a friend who nearly lost a hand –
fighting for freedom?
have you ever seen the face of death
or had to search for the body of a kidnapped friend?
have you ever been laughed at by soldiers
and scared of 'thunder' at night?

251

have you ever marched for what you believe,
have you ever signed a petition, risked arrest?
have you ever sung a song about justice,
have you ever had a friend who wasn't white,
have you ever been on the outside looking in?

have you ever had to deny who you are,
have you ever had to lie for love?
have you ever broken the law just by living,
have you ever been denied your rights?
have they ever tried to cure you of your love?
have you ever thought what it's like being me?

correct me if I'm wrong,
but I think the answer's 'no'
so what makes you
YOU?
tell me
I want to know

Naomi Young
England

Only God to Call on

Some people live in cosy homes
And some sleep on the street.
And some have food put by in tins
And some don't often eat.

Chorus: And some have loved ones standing by
          And some don't have a friend.
          And only God to call on
          Until we make it end.

Some have a cheque book and a card
And some don't have a cent.

Some live in happy marriages.
Some sell themselves for rent.

Some people's mums and dads were kind
And some were very cruel.
And some have work they love to do.
Some never got to school.

Some people have enough to wear
And some cannot get warm.
Some have learned how to cope and some
Put needles in their arm.

Christ knows what it is really like
To be without a friend
And only God to call on
Until we make it end.

Lucy Berry
England

Face to Face

I met her yesterday . . .
inwardly weeping.
You could tell . . .
the depression weighed heavily.
Conscious of the lone silence . . .
she spoke to break the barrier of pain.

I prayed . . .
for the Spirit's anointing.
to refresh and renew . . .
mysteriously as morning dew.

Treasure the developing space –
To be free;
To become.

Simply draw up a chair,
share – face to face
with the only One
In whose image you're made.

Dig deep;
Hold nothing back;
In times of doubt and stress
it's good to talk, watch, wait and listen
to one who knows you well and longs to bless
while you prepare for ultimate wholeness – give.

Wendy Whitehead
England

Stretch Out Your Hand

Endless time to stand and stare
Even tonight in the cold night air;
Stiffly, silently, watching her breath –
Minus possessions
Save blankets for warmth
Plus a prized travel-chess.

Where's she heading?
As if you'd not guess;
Yes, she's but one
Of this world's homeless,
Totally oblivious of time,
Shabby, lonely, resigned.

Her cultured voice is no surprise
A bottle beside her – to idolise;
Standing, waiting – inwardly weeping
As ailing body that bears many a scar
So much for social justice
With every freedom – to frequent the bar!

Now – let me stretch out my hand to you
Be assured, times are changing
On the horizon of hope
The Holy Spirit's engaging
Her powers to renew –
With friends about to embrace; welcome; rescue;
Heralding peace as a dove – miraculously healing,
Steering away from the artificial and false
So this night in the open,
Please God, could well be your last
As each cardboard city collapses in ruins –
A thing of the past!

Wendy Whitehead
England

See, the Man
(John 19.5)

We scrutinise people facing death,
like strange new specimens
of disease, starvation, violence, injustice.

Someone slugged by the humiliating weight
struggling and staggering blindly –
the screen records their desperate oddity.

This one has a breathing-space,
is fully conscious, eating, sleeping,
getting dressed normally, speaking,
standing, sitting or touching normally,
almost like any other time
except for this total relocation
to where death and life cohabit.

And here are some others. Their journeys
(quick or slow, hard or easy?)

are a pilgrimage towards who they are,
and at moments they turn to face us
and be recognised for the first time.

See the men, see the women.
See the Man.

Geoffrey Herbert
England

Blessed Are the Poor

'Beggars' is what he said,
but waxed jackets have no street cred:
I can't beg driving by in my car,
from in there no one'll hear
'Can you spare any change
to help me change gear?'
I won't be fed until I'm starving,
I won't get God's wages until I'm broke,
I won't get any change until I change gear.

How do we get into begging mode?
Do we have to stop laughing
                    stop shopping
                    stop internetting?

Ignatius says, 'Beseech the Lord
to make you completely poor.
Perhaps he will, perhaps he won't – the prayer
will help you to care and not to care.'

Will I learn by meditation,
by a seismic shift of spiritual direction,
by finding what *Ash Wednesday* really means,
by a word of wisdom spilling all my beans?

I want to learn this beggary,
to get guidance on real poverty,
how to sit in humility
ignored by people like me.

What shall I do with my degrees,
all those anxieties,
my personal superiorities?
How do I give up my fear?
How do I change gear?

Geoffrey Herbert
England

Left Alone

Left to manage,
nobody else noticed,
And God where were you?
Left to suffer alone,
nobody else cared,
And God where were you?
Left to endure alone,
nobody else supported,
And God where were you?
Left to cope alone,
nobody else befriended,
And God where were you?
Left to reflect all alone,
Nobody else shared,
And God, where were you?

Frances Ballantyne
England

Come In, Angel

I could not see any wings.
What, no wings?

She wore a long dark coat
that looked a generation old,
with many stains,
and a pullover beneath
in a muddy sort of pink.
Her hair, untidy, dark,
and her skin weather-beaten.
She wanted to sell me
bright yellow plastic mugs
which are not my sort of thing at all.

A clear 'No thank you' seemed right
except – just a look,
a hint of a smile, a plea in her look;
her presence, a plea.
but no wings.

O no-wings angel,
how can I recognise you?
What is the password?
        'I am in need
        and you can help.'
Did I hear that
when you stumbled under the cross?

Bernard Thorogood
Australia

Outcast

Outcast.
Cast out.
Cast away
and sent into the desert,
because they don't fit in
to our strait-jacketed concepts
of who is 'in' and
who is 'out'.

Deserted.
Left to struggle on
their own.
Pushed to the very edge –
and then sometimes over –
by unbearable pressures.

When will our clouded vision
clear?
When will we truly see?
When will we feel
in our very soul,
that an offence
to you
is an indictment
to me.

Susan Hardwick
England

The Outcast

A hand stretched out
to touch the upturned face,
which lit up with surprise and delight.
Others were reluctant to touch him;

they drew back in fear and disgust,
lest they too should share his fate.
To be a leper
was to know rejection and condemnation,
to be cast out from society.
This stranger expressed compassion
and showed no fear.
His touch brought hope and healing.

If more people lost their fear and
followed the example of that stranger,
stretched out hands to touch and welcome,
stood alongside the outcasts,
our world would be a place
of greater hope and happiness.

John Johansen-Berg
England

Jesus Talked with Gentiles

Jesus talked with Gentiles,
  shook the status quo;
praised a Roman captain
  though he was a foe.

Jesus played with children,
  shook the status quo;
criticised disciples
when they cried out, 'No!'

Jesus touched the scabby,
  shook the status quo;
and he healed a blind man
  down in Jericho.

Jesus honoured women,
  shook the status quo;

took them from the kitchen,
put them in the know.

Jesus ate with outcasts,
shook the status quo;
told the sinners, 'Welcome!',
told the righteous, 'Woe!'

Jesus mixed with all sorts,
shook the status quo:
All our cruel exclusions
finally have to go!

Tune: North Coates

Kim Fabricius
England

Together We're Stronger

In a tiny remote village in north Maharashtra state just below the hills which divide this state from Madhya Pradesh, India, Drs Sunil and Shyamala Anand have dedicated their lives to the work of The Leprosy Mission (TLM). This area had suffered a massive famine more than a century ago and subsequently the barren land was given to TLM in order to keep leprosy segregated from the rest of the population. Now, however, the story is different – the centre at Kothara has achieved a reputation of excellence particularly for the eye care and dermatology services on offer to general patients. The new community hospital opened in 2001 made affordable health care available to non-leprosy patients which helped to decrease the stigma associated with leprosy.

All patients sit side by side irrespective of their ailments.

When faced with the realities of life in rural India and the poverty which prevails, any problems in this country (UK) fade into insignificance and it is realised how much is taken for granted. Millions of people in India do not have enough money to feed and clothe their children so paying for health care is low on their list of priorities.

All skin conditions are treated, eye care work is undertaken and many people are referred for eye surgery. Well over a thousand cataract operations are performed every year. The latest service is eye testing and the supply of prescription-made spectacles. The facilities are certainly not state of the art like those in our high-street opticians but the end product is every bit as good and costs a fraction of the price.

and there's more . . .

Recently ten volunteers from Jersey spent a few weeks helping to build an opthalmic suite at Kothara, thanks to a grant given by the government of Jersey. The team described the month as 'unforgettable' and said: 'There is a place in all our hearts for Kothara.' Their rapport with the Indian construction workers was such that they were sad to see the work party depart! In fact, as the group left they were already pencilling a return date for the inauguration ceremony in their diaries.

The Leprosy Mission
England/India

Steadfast Love, Justice and Righteousness
(Based on Luke 9.26–31, 35, 38; Jeremiah 9.24)

Send us, Lord . . .

To the unclothed,
Exposed
For all the world to see;
Object of ridicule,
Contempt –
Unloved.

Grant us steadfast love, justice and righteousness.

To the imprisoned,
Chained
From all the world in darkness,
Forgotten object,
Ignored,
Living death –
Hope lost.

Grant us steadfast love, justice and righteousness.

To the isolated,
Driven
Away from the world;
Object of curiosity,
Dismissed
And overlooked –
Helpless.

Grant us steadfast love, justice and righteousness.

Let your people
Be ours.
Let our glory
Be the cross.

Help us, like Christ,
To reach out –
Speak a word,
Do a deed
Of freedom,
Deliverance,
Giving voice and name
To the voiceless and nameless.
No longer
Unclothed,
Imprisoned.
Isolated,

For God has done much
Through us, in Christ Jesus.

Grant us steadfast love, justice and righteousness.

Claire Smith
Guyana

Who?

Who is the man who sits on the wall
Watching the world
Ignore him?
Where are his people
His flesh,
His being –
Did he leave or did they?
Is that his whole life
Contained in the bag at his feet
So grubby and grey,
And where will he lay
His bearded head tonight?
Did he take flight from the world
And choose to look on
Apart?

He watches and misses no moment –
Anonymous bustlers
Ignore him –
But for the child who tumbles and trips,
And cries out with fear
As he stumbles and falls . . .
He would never be noticed at all.

For the child gives him life
And he leaps up with grace
To raise up the child,

And to look in his face
And to smile . . .

And the smile is of God.

Margot Arthurton
England

Who's That?

Tinker, tailor, soldier, terrorist,
rich man, poor man, asylum seeker, refugee.

Who's that trying to cross the border?
Who's that waiting at the door?
Who's that queuing up for visas?
Who's that sleeping on the floor?

Who's that working in the fields?
Who's that counting out the rent?
Who's that dead in a container,
all the family money spent?

Who's that signing a petition?
Who's that spraying 'Niggers out'?
Who's that moaning about claimants,
while UK tax laws you flout?

Who's that running the soup kitchen,
Who's that challenging the law?
Who's that welcoming the stranger?
Who's that standing by the poor?

Tinker, tailor, soldier, terrorist,
rich man, poor man, asylum seeker, refugee.
Which one could be me?

Janet Lees
England

What a Prospect!

Once he had a job, a good one,
But then the pit had closed,
Shortly before his little accident.
Now no-one wanted to know.
His skill and experience counted for nothing;
His damaged arm closed off ways forward.
As the past was a closed book,
the future was a bleak prospect.
Now he had to manage on allowances and hand-outs,
a grim experience
for someone who had always earned his keep.

His is not an untypical story.
There are many rejects in our communities;
many pockets of poverty in our rich society,
many songs of sorrow and lament
amidst the constant celebrations.
There are ways forward to a better future,
given a political and popular will.
We can plan for society
in which every person, skilled or unskilled,
able-bodied or disabled, young or old,
will have a citizen's income guaranteed
and share in the general welfare
without worry or anxiety or poverty,
making a creative contribution
to a fair and just society.

John Johansen-Berg
England

Margaret of Cortona
(Single Mother)

Margaret of Cortona knew
suffering, and slander, too.

When her lover died, she gave
herself to charity and grave

counsel; worked to keep in bread
the son born out of wedlock's bed

and her penitent self, who knew
hardship enough; the malice, too

in their hearts who doubted the
penitent's sincerity.

Her effect on those around her
showed no heart-change could be sounder.

Margaret of Cortona knew
the God who deems the damnedest true.

Brian Louis Pearce
England

Who Will Speak if We Don't?

Leader: Who will speak if we don't?
Who will speak if we don't?
Who will speak so their voice will be heard?

All: **Who will speak if we don't?**
Who will speak if we don't?
Who will speak so their voice will be heard?

Leader:	Who will speak for the poor and the lonely? Who will speak for the people's oppressed? Who will speak so their voice will be heard? Oh who will speak if we don't?
All:	Who will speak for the poor and the lonely? Who will speak for the peoples oppressed? Who will speak so their voice will be heard? Oh who will speak if we don't?
Leader:	Who will speak for the women and children? Who will speak for the people displaced? Who will speak so their voice will be heard? Oh who will speak if we don't?
All:	**Who will speak if we don't?** **Who will speak if we don't?** **Who will speak so their voice will be heard?** **Oh who will speak if we don't?**

National Council of Churches
Australia

Take Our Disorientation

Take our disorientation
and lead us on our way.
Take our prejudices
and fill them with an open mind and trust.
Take our selfishness
and fill it with compassion and solidarity.
Take our greed
and open our hands to give.
Take our fear
and fill it with courage and confidence.
Take our wrath
and fill it with righteous anger
In front of the powers of injustice.

Carry us into the arms
of faith, hope and love,
the arms of you,
being vulnerable, true and alive
in our world today.

Per Harling
Sweden

Christian Communication

In the depths of silence
no words are needed,
no language required
In the depths of silence
I am called to listen.

Yes, there I sat,
there in that corner,
listening for silence,
longing for community.

Suddenly the room is crowded,
crowded with speeches
voices in many languages
announcing
denouncing
proclaiming
demanding
self-justifying
shattering the silence.
Christian communication must announce,
No, Christian communication must denounce,
No, Christian communication must promote sharing,
No, Christian communication must create community,
Yes, it must have integrity
No, it must call for response.

Please stop, please!
Silence!
Listen to the beating of your heart.
Listen to the blowing of the wind,
the movement of the Spirit.
Be silent said the Lord,
and know that I am God.

And listen to the cry of the voiceless.
Listen to the groaning of the hungry.
Listen to the sigh of the oppressed
and to the laughter of children.

For that is authentic communication:
listening to the people
living with the people
dying with the people.

Anonymous

Minister Reaches Out

The Rev. Charles runs the Ministry to Chennai Eunuchs in the Madras Diocese of the Church of South India. He considers that the church should treat transgendered people* as being made in the image of God, just like any other human being and calls on Christians to provide community support for these people.

He asks people to talk to them freely as when speaking with other people. Try to understand their difficulties. Offer a coffee or a small gift and simply tell them that they are respected.

Transgendered people are often rejected by their families and society, in general. They find it hard to earn a living and some are driven to suicide. Many of these people resort to commercial sex work or sell alcohol and drugs illegally.

The Ministry to Chennai Eunuchs offers transgendered people friendship and support through counselling and

* For transgendered people the gender assigned to them at birth does not reflect the way they feel. Transgender is a term that includes transvestites, transsexuals and cross-dressers.

activities such as yoga classes. They are invited to social and church events and encouraged to accept the Christian faith. So far five people have been baptised as a result of this ministry.

Council for World Mission/Geoffrey Duncan
South India/England

Migrant

She was lured
by an astute recruiter,
who promised
she will work as a hairdresser –
She ends up
at a brothel, a sex worker.

She refused;
no one listened to her objection.
Instead she
was battered into submission.
And threatened –
More protests and she'd be bludgeoned.

A migrant –
Stranger in a foreign land;
She's forlorn.
she's to follow the boss's command
and fulfil
what her customers would demand.

There's no one
to help and come to her rescue.
All day long
she serves men, young and old, old and new.
When alone,
she sits in a room without a view.

She's hungry.
Each days she eats only kaotom.*
She's sick
by men who refuse to wear a condom.
She longs for
affection and for freedom.

Is there hope
for her and for countless others;
Innocent
children sold to heartless slavers;
Redemption
so remote, suffering forever?

It's karma,
they tell her, due to her past deeds.
Such nonsense!
This is human cruelty and greed.
No! Never
what the Almighty has decreed!

O where's God?
On her knees she asks day and night,
begging God
to liberate her and others with God's might –
The children
and women who dwell in the night.

Salvador T. Martinez
Thailand

Angela's Story

Angela Thakuri is 57 years old. Her life is just one example of the ongoing struggle of leprosy. The rejection and shame she feels is real and carved deeply into her life. Yet, at The Leprosy Mission (TLM) hospital in Kolkata, India she has found new

---

* kaotom is boiled rice.

friends . . . nurses and doctors who care for her like Christ cared for the sick, the lame and the blind.

When Angela told her story she was very sick. Jaundiced and suffering from hepatitis B did not make her struggle any easier.

Angela tells:

I was born in Kolkata in 1946. I was a telephone operator and then became a teacher when I was about thirty-five. About that time I found patches on my skin. I went to the doctor but no one even suspected leprosy – except one. But when he realised that I may have leprosy, he simply walked away.

My illness took a dramatic turn for the worse. I became very sick and couldn't find relief from a fever for two months. I was taken to the government hospital at Darjeeling. A German doctor recognised the symptoms of leprosy and sent me to TLM Kolkata for full diagnosis. I had leprosy.

My friends and relatives in Kolkata were frightened and the stigma of leprosy kept them from seeing me. My brother refused to have anything to do with me – he won't even come and visit. So, I was admitted to the hospital as an inpatient.

The Leprosy Mission hospital is so good. The doctors and nurses here take great care of me. I feel at home.

The Leprosy Mission
England/India

We Confess Our Failings in Community

We confess our failings in community:
Our lack of understanding,
Our lack of forgiveness,
Our lack of openness,
Our lack of sensitivity.
We confess the times:
When we are too eager to do better than others,
When we are too rushed to care,

273

When we are too tired to bother,
When we are too lazy to really listen,
When we are too quick to act from motives other than
    love.

All: **We seek the forgiveness of God and of each other.**

Corrymela Community
Northern Ireland

This Is Christmas

Bright lights blazing, garish colours.
'MERRY CHRISTMAS' on neon signs.
Illumined streets, shops, trees,
churches whose notice-boards,
with Christ child's shrine,
proclaim in letters three feet high,
'CHRIST COMES – THE LIGHT OF THE WORLD.'

He doesn't come here,
beyond the edge,
into this darkness.

Bright greetings cards, cosy firesides.
Cotton wool sheep, rustic stables,
skaters, robins, Old Man Christmas,
camels, crackers, laden tables,
eighteenth-century Arcadia.
'CHRIST COMES – THE GOOD SHEPHERD.'

He doesn't come here,
beyond the margin,
into the hopelessness.

Bright homes prepared for parties.
Families round their Christmas trees.
Office 'do's' and get-togethers.
Gifts exchanged – warmth, comfort, ease.

Carollers singing round a crib.
'CHRIST IS BORN – AND LIVES AMONG US.'
'HE IS LOVE. HE IS LOVE!'

So where is love out here,
in the cold,
ISOLATED?

THIS IS CHRISMAS.
THIS IS CHRISTMAS
AND EVERY DAY
FOR THOUSANDS LIKE ME.
THIS IS CHRISTMAS.

Jessica Isherwood
England

Disturb Me

Disturb me Lord,
Disturb me until I cannot stand;
until I cannot think,
until I cannot pray.
Disturb me until I am still enough to rest in your presence.
Only then will I not be disturbed by those I do not
    understand;
those I am frightened of,
those I feel threatened by.
Transform me, Lord,
and send me out in your service
to disturb others in Christ's name
until we are disturbed enough to stand together.

Lynne Chitty
England

You May Cry

You *may* cry.
You *may* be afraid.
You *may* feel small.
You *may* feel abandoned.
You *may* despair.
It is alright to be a vulnerable person.
But don't be shameful,
don't feel guilty.
It is not *your* fault.
It *is* not your fault.
It is *not* your fault.
One day you will leave
all these hard things behind you.
You will get help.
You will be able
to love yourself again.
            It will be fine,
            fine, fine . . .

Per Harling
Sweden

Note from God

When they cut the cord
and branded you bastard
I was there.

When your father left,
when your mother wept,
I was there.

When she turned
to her brother for comfort
I was there.

I was in
Your mother's arms
Your uncle's eyes –

I was the porch light,
the place at table,
the bed where they laid you.

I took you in
I was there.

Denise Bennett
England

This Is Real

I've not the words to say proper
how I sometime feel
but I do know what is right
what is real. Or
when someone is just making fun,
call me rude name,
unzip my bag tip it run.
Won't wait for s.l.o.w. . .e.a.s.y. . .w.o.r.d.s
that they learnt long ago.
Ride on the *special* bus
so now everybody know,
I've not the words to say proper
how I sometime feel,
but I do know what is right
what is real.

Come to my party. Be the star turn.
Shout my name loud. Feel my face burn,
Play inside not outside
safe is not such fun,
playing my own game
pretending I have won.

Mum and Dad pick up pieces I forget to hold,
carry my bag of words – some I've not been told.
They say I'm a good person and God know how I feel,
I know that must be right, because I know that God is real.

Eve Jackson
England

Dis-Illusioned

I feel the wind floating through my words
I feel the wind speaking with emotion
I see the rain falling so soft from the sky
I see the rain stop and feel a loved one's cry
I feel a soft petal fall from a fresh rose
I imagine all animals just let free
Running through the meadows.
I feel tensed and so warm until I get this shiver
Now I feel cold and lonely and it's making me quiver
I see everyone running and walking out of my life
I feel the rain fall so hard and see the pages
And chapters of my life walking away
I can't walk with liberty no more because it walks
Alone
I feel so sad and unhappy inside I feel like the deserts
Lost without sand
I walk in the dark all alone with my life
To spare
I'm all wet from the rain and my face is moist with tears
I've only just found out
After all these years
That nobody loves me
But everybody fears.

***

Dear O Mighty God
I pray today for someone to understand
To love me
And to begin the story of my life
And to realise how much I've struggled
And how hard it is
And how hard it has been
To reach so far in life.
So I pray to you today
To spread my words around the world.
Amen xxx

Zola F.
England

The Denial of Christ – From Whom Do We Deny Wholeness?

The setting is a single candle on a purple cloth in the central position of the worship space. Images of war, poverty, homelessness, tears below the candle . . .

Call to Worship: Let us come into the place and listen for the voice of God.

Reading: Luke 22.3–6

Sung Response: Jesus Christ, Son of God, have mercy on us (or another suitable song/hymn)

Leader: Great Creator Spirit we confess that we often wish you would go away.
We hide from your voice and your guidance.
We want to change the world to suit us.
We want to ignore the bits of the world that challenge our lifestyle,
and we forget that it is your creation and your will to be done.

Voice One:	Where are the homeless people in our city, Surely they can help themselves?
Voice Two:	Who is excluded from our community, Everyone is welcome, it's up to them to make the effort to fit in.
Voice Three:	The government will look after the environment Where does God call me to 'save the trees'?
Reading:	Luke 22.31–34
Leader:	Great Creator Spirit we confess that we often try hard to serve you We try with the best intentions to do what you ask But sometimes when the time comes, our courage fails us, And we step away from what we know to be truth. Great Creator Spirit forgive us, when we fail to notice; When we think we know best about ourselves and your creation; When we fail to live out our commitment to you; When we do not recognise the pain in our society, and fail to find ways to help; When we do not recognise our own pain, and our need for healing. Have mercy on us, Son of God, as we seek to be your people in this place. Amen
Sung Response:	– free choice

280

Reading:	Luke 22.47–62
Leader:	We all have experiences like Peter at some time or another.
	A time when we promised to do something and didn't.
	A commitment we made to change the way we lived and didn't.
	A time when we have ignored what is happening around us because it was easier.

As a Christian community we say we are committed to challenging injustice in the community, to standing with the poor and the oppressed, to bringing about transformation in the world. But this is often hard. We would rather that the Church, or we ourselves, did not act. We do not want to be controversial, or we do not have time, or we are frightened about what people might think, or we don't want to give up our power or control, or we just feel powerless or scared.

For whatever reason, there are times in our life where we deny, as Peter did. We deny our true self; deny what we are committed to; deny the giftedness we have; or fail to own our full potential. There are even times when we deny that we belong to the Church, or are a follower of Christ.

Act: Spend some time in silence, and reflect on your experience of denial as an individual or as a community.

When you are ready, I invite you to come forward and light a candle as a symbol of

281

your desire to name Christ as yours; that
you might seek not to deny who you are
as a creation of God, or deny God as the
creator, and that you might seek to live out
in an active way within this community. In
doing so we will shed light onto the images
of struggle in our world and acknowledge
that we are seeking change.

Prayers for those who are denied wholeness

Leader: We pray for those who are denied life,
For those who live in situations of conflict
and persecution.

Silence

We pray for those who are denied hope,
For those who are homeless and live with
the strain of poverty.

Silence

We pray for those who are denied
wholeness,
For those who are lonely and hurting and
have nowhere to turn.

Silence

We pray for ourselves

All: **That we might have the courage to
acknowledge ourselves,
To struggle for a world where all people
are acknowledged,
And where peace is lived out daily.
Amen.**

Voice One:	Let us go out with courage.
Voice Two:	Let us go out with love.
Voice Three:	Let us go out as people with hope.
Together:	**Let us be bold, for we go in the spirit of God.** **Amen**

Christine Cargill
Australia

Let us Pray in the Words of the Psalmist

We remember the refugees, the asylum seekers, the discriminated, the unemployed, the sick, homeless and hungry, the abused and all those crying aloud and in whispers for God's intervention, invoking God's liberating grace, of longing, and of preparedness and hope of those and in solidarity.

How long, O Lord?
Will you forget me forever?
How long will you hide your face from me?
How long must I bear pain in my soul, and have sorrow in my
heart all day long?
How long shall my enemy be exalted over me?
Consider and answer me, O Lord my God!
Give light to my eyes, or I will sleep the sleep of death,
and my enemy will say, 'I have prevailed';
my foes will rejoice because I am shaken.
But I trusted in your steadfast love; my heart shall rejoice in
your salvation.
I will sing to the Lord, because he has dealt bountifully with
me.

Psalm 13

Deenabandhu Manchala
India

283

Magdalene's Business

I was a whore. Was I the only one?
I sold myself. Oh yes. I set the sum.
Unlike the sheltered girls with careful dads
Who totted up the worth of likely lads.

The world was with me always, everywhere.
And would you say you'd never sold yourself?
Watched from the railings while the bully struck?
Hawked friendship round those folk you envied most?
Invested cash in bonds? (And I *mean* bonds).

Business was business. Yes. I was a whore.
And then He came; I'm not one any more.

But since that time of trading all alone,
I'm skilled at spotting other little whores.
And not too quick at casting the first stone.

I've learned to mind my business. Do the same.

Lucy Berry
England

7

A New Heaven on Earth

Come, you that are blessed by my Father, inherit the
kingdom prepared for you from the foundation of the
world.

Matthew 25.34

There is often the need to look beyond and behind words to
discover new revelations and insights into the Kingdom of
Heaven here on earth. There is much to be explored and realized
in relation to Christ here and alongside people in unexpected
places, people and situations. Look in a broad sense for new
ways to worship, new understandings of how people care for
people in our global society.

Pearl Willemssen Hoffmann from the USA expresses her
understanding of the fact that 'We Are All God's Children' (page
287) The writing about the West-Eastern Diwan Orchestra (page
292) in which the distinguished conductor Daniel Barenboim
and historian Edward Said have done so much to promote
peace should receive wide publicity. We need many people to
take on the role of 'Misfit' as written by Bernard Thorogood
from Australia (page **296**). In 'A Quiet Way' by Eve Jackson
(page **299**) is commended for reflection and action, as is 'One
Candle' by Marjorie Dobson (page **302**) and as we look to a
new heaven on earth there is much to consider in Wendy Ross-
Barker's 'God is Really Wonderful' (page **311**). 'Love Is a Key
in a Lock' (page **290**) by Lucy Berry encourages everyone to
'knock on your neighbour's door, or call out from the hall'.

Rainbow Promise

God of the rainbow promise,
light up our world with colour.
May your people of many hues
respond to each other with delight.
May the gifts of the Maoris
be treasured by all Kiwis.
May the creativity of the Inuit people
bring pleasure to all Canadians.
May the Zulus and Afrikaaners
find common ground in celebration.
May the Catholics and Protestants
dance together in a just and peaceful Ireland.
May Tamils and Sinhalese
end the violence and begin a process of reconciliation.
May Russians recognise the rights of Chechens
And Chechens seek the welfare of Russians.
May black and white live in harmony;
may old and young unite in symphony.
May all the varied peoples
celebrate together in our global village,
worshipping the God of all creation.

John Johansen-Berg
England

We Are All God's Children

We are all God's children; each person is created by God.

We are a little lower than the angels.
Yet we are fragile individuals,
Injury or infection in one limb affects the whole person.
We earthlings are linked together in the bond of humanness.
Harm to any individual is injury to all,
Violence to anyone is registered in the invisible spheres.

As humans we have the gift of song;
We sing praises to our Father/Mother God.

As humans we can manifest God's caring love to the
    world.
As a hen gathers her brood under her wings our God protects
    us.
As a shepherd calls his sheep into the fold our God calls us
    unto himself.
As a shepherd pours oil on the wounds his sheep have
    suffered in the pastures,
Our Father/Mother God extends loving care.

The angels call to each of us; the Holy Spirit wants – yes,
    waits – to empower us.
However, like sheep we have gone astray,
We are too concerned with our own welfare,
We do not understand that we are all God's children:
Thousands of children starve while some of us cast out what
    we cannot consume.
We do not provide homes for the homeless:
Yet we strive for bigger and bigger homes for ourselves.
We do not comprehend that we all belong to the human
    race:
That injury and hurt to one human affects us all.

We think we know the mind of God:
We want to decide who should live in this area or that
    land
We do not comprehend that all the earth is the Lord's
And the fullness thereof.

We think we can read the signs:
    Lo, Jesus is coming soon,
    Only some will be taken to glory,
    Only the chosen will see his face.

Do we not understand that all God's children belong to Him,
   That all are chosen to receive His love?

Father, forgive us, we know not what we are doing.

Pearl Willemssen Hoffman
USA

The Church Is Not Confined by Boundaries

I give you a new commandment, that you love one another.
Just as I have loved you, you also should love one another.
By this everyone will know that you are my disciples, if you
   have love for one another.

(John 13.34–35)

The lilac and the hawthorn scents permeate the grey dampness
of an Australian spring morning. A couple of cockatoos squawk
loudly as we drive by on our way to preach at the Springvale
Church of Christ, Melbourne, Australia. We arrived early and
people introduced themselves as they entered the church. Fred
from Germany. Frank comes from Portugal. Daisy's home is in
Kenya. Andrew and Nisha hail from Sudan. Son and his parents emigrated from Vietnam. Forty people gathered for worship but we might as well have been standing in the foyer of the
United Nations rather than in suburban Melbourne. We asked
how many different countries are represented in the Springvale
congregation and an elder replied, 'More than twenty countries
are represented when we gather for worship each week.'

Son, a young adult, left his parents in the pew and slipped
out as we started the sermon. His parents put on headphones.
The sermon was amplified into the narthex where Son sat and
translated it into Vietnamese. His parents heard the Word in
their native tongue.

As communion was served we were reminded that the Church
is not confined by boundaries or national loyalties. Indeed, we
have a higher allegiance to God through Jesus Christ our Lord.
The unity that we feel at the table Jesus has set for us is a unity

that calls us to work for justice and peace. At this communion table in Springvale we were reminded that we are sisters and brothers with all God's people, inside the Church and out, in Australia and internationally.

Ana and Tod Gobledale
Australia/USA

Love Is a Key in a Lock

I have been all alone.
It is almost too hard to bear
To remember that time
When no-one was there:

No-one with keys to my lock.
No-one to open the door.
No-one to call from the hall
Any more.

Now I am not alone.
I know I have been blessed.
I have reasons to get up
And get dressed.

I nod to the ones in the street
The ones who seem so bleak,
Who look as if they have
No reason to speak:

Women who mumble along
Talking to nobody there.
Grey men who gaze from a bench
Into thin air.

Mothers with no-one who'll help.
Fathers with family lost,

Struggling through the hours
At such terrible cost.

Love is a key in a lock.
So if you love people at all,
Knock on your neighbour's door
Or call out from the hall.

Lucy Berry
England

Sparrows

I am driven into the tamed wilderness
outside my back door.

Along the flower beds there are
stones to be turned into bread, and
on the far side of the rhododendrons
a view of all the kingdoms of the earth.
Perhaps I'll be tempted to throw myself
from the pinnacle of the clematis montana
and be caught by angels.

Ethiopians come for the bread,
in the bluebells Iraqis shelter from smart bombs,
and Chechnyans under the ruined squirrel-feeder
yearn for angels to rescue them.

I open my heart to the snail-borne sufferings
among the biochemical pellets,
and pray for a compassion that reaches out
farther than my own larch-lap fence.

This morning I found a man, starving and weak,
cold from being out there all night. He said,
Your wilderness is enough for me to feel

all the sufferings in the galaxies.
I touched him and for a moment I felt them too.

Geoffrey Herbert
England

West-Eastern Diwan Orchestra

This orchestra was founded by the conductor and pianist Daniel Barenboim and the cultural critic and historian, Edward Said. Barenboim is a Jew born in Argentina and Said, who died recently, was a Palestinian born into an Anglican family and brought up in Alexandria, Egypt. It was through their friendship that young Israeli, Arab and German musicians were first brought together in Weimar, Germany in 1999 to play in a concert for the 250th anniversary of the birth of the German poet, Goethe. The orchestra took its name from a set of poems that Goethe wrote which were influenced by his encounter with Islam, the West-Oestlicher Diwan.

The orchestra played, one year, at the London promenade concerts and was the subject of a television documentary. While the news headline at that time spoke about the collapse of the so-called road map to peace in the Middle East, and on a day when there had been yet another suicide bombing in Israel, two young pianists, Saleem Abboud-Ashkar, a Palestinian and Shai Wosner, an Israeli, were taking their bows at the Royal Albert Hall, London UK with Barenboim after a performance of Mozart's Concerto for Three Pianos; they were holding hands as they acknowledged the enthusiastic applause of a capacity audience for an ovation that lasted half an hour.

What the West-Eastern Divan Orchestra project has been able to achieve is to bring together young musicians who would not otherwise have encountered one another across the divisions of faith and politics in the Middle East. They have discovered a common humanity as well as the joy of what it means to make music together. As Barenboim wrote:

292

An Arab boy found himself sharing a desk with an Israeli cellist. They were trying to play the same note, to play with the same dynamic, with the same stroke of the bow, with the same sound, with the same expression. They were trying to do something together, something about which they both cared, about which they were both passionate. Well, having achieved that one note, they already can't look at each other the same way because they have shared a common experience. I believe if only we can foster this kind of contact it can only help people feel nearer to each other, that is all.

John Swarbrick
England

Notes: In Autumn 2004 The Barenboim-Said Foundation opened the first Music Kindergarten in memory of the late Edward Said. Most of the students were from refugee camps around the Ramallah area.

Three London UK ministers have formed a piano trio: cellist, violinist, pianist with the name of Parsons' Noyse. They played recently at Methodist Central Hall London UK when the money raised was given to the West-Eastern Divan Orchestra – another example of angels in today's society.

Yasmin's Rose

They started with the garden:
green vines, reward for years of toil,
crushed, flattened, eliminated
the day the bulldozers came.

The house was next, home to twelve
adults, children, babies – demolished,
reduced to rubble
and with it Yasmin's rose.

293

Bulldozers can't demolish
the spirit of resistance;
soon they rebuilt. See the green shoots
of Yasmin's rose reborn.

Living in a tent all winter
after the next demolition
no fun for anyone, but Yasmin's rose
pushed through the rubble,

a symbol to strengthen their spirits.
Another rebuild soon in place,
the bulldozers came back
yet Yasmin's rose triumphed again.

Now their fourth house half complete
surrounded by desolation
already the demolition order's out
but Yasmin's rose is blooming again.

And if you've wondered why
they need – yes, it really exists –
the Israeli Committee Against
House Demolitions,

well, now you know.

Patricia Price-Tomes
Israel/Palestine/England

Meditation on The Lord's Prayer

Our Father who art in Heaven, you want us your children to build a new earth of sisterhood and brotherhood, not a hell of violence and death.
Holy be your name, that in your name Lord, let there be no abuse, no oppression and no manipulation of the conscience and liberty of your children.

Your Kingdom come, not the kingdom of fear, force or money, of seeking peace through war.

Your will be done on Earth as it is in Heaven, in this land of ours and in sister lands which echo with gunfire and cries of fear.

Give us this day our daily bread, the bread of peace, Lord, so that we can sow our maize and beans, watch them grow and share them together as a family.

Forgive us our sins as we forgive those who sin against us. Do not let our relationships be based on self-interest. Let us change laments for songs of life, clenched fists for outstretched hands and the weeping of widows and orphans for smiles.

Lead us not into temptation, the temptation to conform, to do nothing: the temptation not to collaborate with you in the search for justice and peace.

But deliver us from evil, from behaving like Cain to our brothers and sisters, from believing ourselves rulers over life and death.

For yours is the Kingdom, the Power and the Glory. You are our hope of salvation, in you we place our trust.

Group of Refugees
El Salvador

The Lonely Lord's Prayer

Our Father
who came to the least
who art in heaven
yet wept for the lonely
hallowed be thy name
for your name is called
thy kingdom come
from the edge of this world
thy will be done
where the lost and the empty

on earth
and the marginalised gather
as it is in heaven
knowing no hope
give us this day our daily bread
forgotten, unknown
and forgive us our trespasses
we expect no more
as we forgive those
and hold out hands to those
who trespass
who cut us down
against us
when in their path
and lead us not into temptation
as we look on knowing
but deliver us from evil
we are not worthy
for thine is the kingdom
for here on the edge are
the power and the glory
those forgotten by God
forever and ever
or his people
amen
it seems

Duncan L. Tuck
England

Misfit

Yes, I'm a misfit.
I tramp the roads,
and when they ask me for my address
I say, 'Somewhere between Ballarat and Bendigo.'
I sleep under southern stars
and know the sweetness of stolen morning milk.

Yes, I'm a misfit
with my crooked back and limping walk,
I move awkwardly and stand leaning,
so people look at me and look away,
wondering if I am drunk.

I suppose I'm a misfit
because I dream so much
and can't keep to regular hours.
I have these brilliant dreams
and try to express them in paint,
but no one seems to understand.

You could call me a misfit,
for I went into business as a Christian
determined not to fudge or bully
or do other people down
or cut corners to make more profit.
and I found that I was alone.

God made me a misfit
when I put my arms around that addict,
and I found that I loved those
strugglers with drugs.

Come with me all misfits,
for I am not of the established order,
and my way is not traditional
and my family don't understand me,
and all the authorities call me a rebel.
I am the man outside the door.
I know loneliness too.

Come with me
and we will make
a new community.

Bernard Thorogood
Australia

A Creed

We believe in a community that opens its doors
    to people who flee war, hunger and poverty
    in search of a better life.

We believe in the power of love, not the power of violence.

We believe that we are called to share our lives
    so as to free each other from poverty, racism
    and oppression of all kinds.

We believe that the resources of the earth
    are to be shared among all people –
    not just the few.

We believe in a community that has as a priority
    a response to those who are denied
    basic human rights and dignity.

We reject a world where people are denied access to warmth,
    food, shelter and the right to live in peace.

We want to believe in justice, in goodness and in people.

We believe we are called to a life of freedom,
    of service,
    of witness,
    of hope.

We reject the idea that nothing can be done.

We believe that a time will come when all people
    will share in the richness of our world,
    and that all people will be truly loved and respected.

We commit ourselves in the name of God
    who created the world for all to share,

of Christ who leads us to freedom, and
of the Spirit who calls us to action.

Today we commit ourselves to work together
to make this belief a reality.

CAFOD
England

In a Quiet Way

If I am to find you
in the simplest of tasks
the quietest of ways,
I too must learn to walk
with a humble presence
through my days –

    the quiet not becoming
    a silence of power
    a stunning of sound,
    the stifling murmur of past
    thinking itself into heavily bound.

I cannot shake collection plates like tambourines,
or dress your image in handsome riches,
nor be that gathered crowd before a throne.
For me, it is sensing your smallness;
a reachable presence when I am alone.

Your mystery is hidden in my creation
and is the 'doing' of an ordinary day.
My *stillness* is where your love is at work
moulding me to your shape and your way.

Eve Jackson
England

How Odd of God
(based on Acts 12.1–17)

'It's Peter! It's Peter! He's alright!'
'He can't be alright, we've been praying for him.'

Of course, Peter was alright and Rhoda knew what she was talking about. But people would surely remember her harmless lapse – leaving him at the door like that. Perhaps it was characteristic, maybe she was a bit scatty, prone to be absent-minded. At any rate the story would be told of her, long after Peter had been spirited away to a safer place. 'Rhoda, she's the one who left Peter standing outside.'

A word in defence of Rhoda. She left Peter standing there because she was so delighted at his freedom, brought practically out of death and back to life. And people who remembered her absent-mindedness would remember too what had made her so excited and what an amazing night it had been.

Rhoda is you and me. Whether we mean to or not, we share God's good news in ways that reflect our own personality and our own foibles. We tell of Jesus being brought from death to life, in ways that show what we are like too. Rhoda was so stirred and moved by her message, that people surely remembered not just her way of telling it – odd as that was – but the message she had brought. Maybe Rhoda wasn't too bad a preacher after all. When she had news to tell, her own personality was part of the telling.

Lord, we offer you lives and love, faith and hope. And you take us as we are. By the gentle yet relentless pressure of your Holy Spirit, you shape us after the pattern of Christ. And by the holy optimism that is your right and purpose, you mean to use us to praise, serve and proclaim you. Thank you, Lord God, through Jesus Christ our Lord. Amen.

John Proctor
England

You Made the Earth

For the richness of the harvest
And the gifts of your creation
We praise you Lord

**Response: You made the earth
             And saw that it was good**

For the smiles of your children
And the beauty of your people
We praise you Lord

**Response: You made the earth
             And saw that it was good**

For the chance to share with others
And to celebrate your glory
We praise you, Lord

**Response: You made the earth
             And saw that it was good**

Linda Jones/CAFOD
England

Resolutions for the Twenty-first Century

In the future that we live together, we will begin again,
We will feed the hungry, we will turn,
To everyone in need,
We will share the world's resources; we will turn away from
  greed.
And we will learn to love.

We will learn to look beyond the colour of a skin,
We will learn to find the things that make the whole world
  kin,

We will learn to see,
The whole wide world all as one family,
And we will treat them all with love.

We choose building in place of destroying, forgiveness
    instead of hating,
We choose peace instead of killing,
We will make a fuller life,
We choose life, peace and forgiveness,
Above all we choose love.

Doreen Gazey
England

One Candle

One candle doesn't do much.
Lights up a small corner.
But only just!

One prayer doesn't say much.
Shows concern for a while.
But not for long!

One Christian doesn't achieve much.
Works until empty.
But without much hope!

One voice . . .
. . . but surely there is more than one?
One and one and one and one,
that's four already!

Multiply again and again
and again;
soon there are hundreds, thousands, millions!

One million candles
can light ten thousand rooms.

One million prayers
can transform concern into action.

One million Christians
can . . . ?

Can't we?

Marjorie Dobson
England

Hill of Harmony
An Event at Corrymeela

It's raining on the Hill of Harmony
But soon there's a rainbow in the sky
And everyone is smiling . . .

'Entertaining Strangers' is our theme;
As we struggle to honour our differences,
But often fail . . .

Sacred writings from many traditions
Tell us not to be afraid;
But we are . . .

We look at why this is,
And are encouraged to face our fear,
But find it hard . . .

Early years of admonition –
'Beware of strangers'
Holds us back . . .

We learn that befriending strangers
IS the spiritual journey,
It is the way to live . . .

We come away 'transformed'.
This gives us strength
To walk the Pilgrim Way.

Our insights and our self-evaluation
Have helped us to experience the 'Divine'
And made sense of our existence. Hallelujah!

Nia Rhosier
Wales

Just imagine . . .

an image of your God . . .

. . . as your own safe place . . .

. . . in a busy city of ideas . . .

. . . a sign to follow . . .

. . . a road to walk along . . .

. . . a corner to turn . . .

. . . a path to explore . . .

. . . a door to open . . .

. . . a light in a room . . .

. . . a warmth by a fire . . .

. . . the safe place in your life . . .

. . . to find your God waiting.

Eve Jackson
England

The Waiting Time

In the beginning, God waited . . .
waited for the dark earth to turn sunwards
for sky and sea to divide and land to rise from the water;
waited for the trees to grow green
and living creatures to leap and swim and fly
and at last for his children to be born –
the apples of his eye
and partners in his creation.

Beyond the beginning, God waits . . .
cherishing his vision for humanity –
while the devious and destructive children
trample across the world shouting obscenities.
Spoil for a fight rather than seeking friendship,
grab at his gifts, and toss them aside, abused and broken.

God-in-waiting, we turn to you,
Despite our deep disgrace, you wait with outstretched
    arms.
Help us to lay aside the childishness
that stunts our growth and spoils your vision for us.
Come close to us so we can whisper to you
the secrets we dare not confess to others,
and through your forgiveness make us joyful.

Give each one of us new energy and resolve
to build communities where people live in harmony.
Persuade us that a waiting time is an expectant time –
a time not for entrenchment but for restoration.
In the face of uncontrollable aggression,
the threat of terror and the mirages of madness –
give us courage and determination
to hold fast to our faith, believing in your promise
that, at the time you choose,

all creation, once again,
will cross the threshold of your Kingdom.

Jill Jenkins
England*

Exciting God

Exciting God, we pray for those people of vision and initiative
who place new challenges before us
and encourage us to catch their vision.
That is not always easy
and we do not necessarily greet these ideas with enthusiasm.
Forgive us our lack of courage.
Fire our imaginations.
Teach us to be more like those first disciples of Jesus
who had no idea what to expect,
yet were prepared to attempt to follow their calling.
Excite us with your vision of your kingdom come on earth –
Through the work that we do as Christians.

*Marjorie Dobson
England*

A New Heaven on Earth

From Alpha to Omega
to Alpha –
from beginning to end
and so
back to the beginning again.
From the moment
you created
to the second you summoned
its return,
the pendulous world
wildly and wantonly

306

swung and spun first
one way then
the other –
from your wish and will
to ours –
then inexorably back again.

Creator God –
how you must adore all
that you have made
to endure
so patiently and so long
all our endeavour
to destroy.

Yet you *will* prevail –
I know you will –
for it is Your Will.
You are Alpha
and Omega
and Alpha:
The Beginning
and The End
and The Beginning Again.

Susan Hardwick
England

Empowering God, Dynamic Christ

Empowering God, Dynamic Christ,
Who calls our sleeping souls to wake,
With potent devastating love
Our smug self-satisfaction shake.

Our grasping hands presume to take
More than we need to live in health;
We plunder and pollute the earth,
Tight fisted, portion out its wealth.

Two thousand years have seen the wrongs
Perpetuated down the years,
Ignoring each distressing cry
We do not heed the victim's tears.

So babies still are born in caves,
And refugees beg for a crust,
As still the world is run for gain,
And we give only when we must.

O God, forgive our ravenous greed,
Our spirit's abject poverty,
O melt our hearts and make us see
Your Love is our security.

Help us renounce the world's false charms,
Its frantic haste, its values cold,
As we embrace Your simple law
To love our neighbours more than gold.

So may Your Love sign all our cheques,
And may our open hearts employ
The boundless Love we see in Christ
To give, and share our best with joy.

Till poor in property and pride,
And rich in Love and Peace and Grace,
Abundance flows from every heart
Transforming all the human race.

Christine E. Collin
England

A Prayer for the Church

Bless you, Wise and Holy One,
    for your call to be
    your Word-made-flesh
    in the world.

Enable us to be
  a church that dares to seek justice
  where others fear to tread;
  a church that cares
  not just for its own kind
  but for animal, plant, and planet, too;
  a church that has the grace
  to admit its mistakes – and the wisdom
  to learn from them.
Inspire us to be
  not a church that blindly follows
  in the footsteps of Jesus
  but one that seeks what he sought –
    how to seek justice
    without sacrificing mercy;
    how to keep the peace
    without sacrificing the truth;
    how to be loving
    without counting the cost
    to ourselves.
Bless you, Wise and Holy One,
  for your high calling
  to be *your* church
  in *your* world.

  Amen

Norm S. D. Esdon
Canada

Imagine

Imagine   Imagine
a death sentence   a drug
on a civil servant's whim   you could afford
initiated by your husband   a government
the soldier   who told you
bringing his work home   how to protect yourself
sharing it with you   to save your children

Imagine
a death sentence
metered out by
family and friends
turning their back on you
the modern day
stoning in the village

Imagine
a death sentence
hanging over you
written in long words
you don't understand
pandered to by white coats
who can't take it away

Imagine this
her name is Destiny
for millions of women
in Africa

Imagine
that people didn't whisper
behind your back
that knowledge was power
that all wanted to share
that you are the same as me
with equal right to care

Imagine
they didn't say
it was your fault
that you loved the wrong way
the wrong one
that you liked needles too much
and careless living

Imagine this
his name is Fantasy
yes, sometimes
even here

Naomi Young
England

Entertaining Angels

I believe that angels are all around
I believe that angels entertain your mind
when you are all alone.
Angels are a gift from heaven,
they comfort you on rainy days.
I believe that if you see an angel you will
walk in liberty for the rest of your life.
I believe angels come to see those who are
special and work hard for a living
For those who have not seen an angel your
time will come.

I believe there is more than one angel.
But there is one special angel that lives in
the heart of every one and she's an
Entertaining Angel.

Zola F.
England

God Is Really Wonderful!

Life was good for Sahr. He had been training as a nurse at the Nixon Memorial Hospital in Sierra Leone. By now, he had reached the stage where he was entrusted with the responsibility of running a clinic in one of the small towns. He enjoyed his work and felt good about being able to care for people who were ill. He was also a member of the Methodist Youth Fellowship, delighting in its activities and the worship of the church. It was this which led to a very special opportunity. He was chosen as a member of a Youth Exchange Team, which was to go to England that year. A team from Liverpool had already visited Sierra Leone and been overwhelmed by the welcome they had received. Now they were preparing for their visitors to come to them.

Then things changed in Sierra Leone. The trouble in Liberia spilled across the border, where people had been giving hospitality to refugees. Homes were looted, people were wounded and killed. Others fled for their lives. Sahr's clinic was destroyed and he had to go into hiding in the bush, along with many others. In spite of it all he was brought to safety and with the rest of the team was able to come to England.

On returning home he went back to the clinic. In a letter he wrote, 'I found nothing'.

People needed the care he could offer so the clinic was set up again. But the peace had gone from Sierra Leone and the following years were full of unrest as civil war developed. Nobody in the areas of conflict was safe. Sahr lost his clinic again and fled. Eventually he made his way back to the hospital. He wrote to say that as he fled he had gone from village to village preaching

311

the gospel. The pattern was repeated and in one attack the hospital itself was ransacked. In spite of it all, Sahr refused to despair. He was accepted as a non-stipendiary minister of the Methodist Church of Sierra Leone. His letters told of loss, of fleeing for his life, of going into hiding in the bush. Yet mingled in the story there is to be found the repeated exclamation that 'God is really wonderful'.

Wendy Ross-Barker
England

The Lover's Response

It's hard for me to say this although it's coming
from the heart
I didn't think I would feel this way although I
felt it at the start.

You made me feel special like I'd never felt this way
before
It was destiny when you loved me because I've loved
you ever more.

I would never hurt you never spite the way
others feel
Because now we are together I know the love
we show is real.

If ever you was to leave me it would never
feel the same
I could never picture myself calling another
lover's name.

I'm so glad to be with you and I hope you feel
the same
Because the love I give and show to you
hurts me
like a pain.

Zola F.
England

Earth = Heaven

Earth = heaven?
Is this the equation?
Is it possible?

Am I deluded to think it possible,
and the moments when I say 'yes',
afraid to share the vision?
Earth = heaven

Beyond the inhumanity,
behind the isolation,
back of the inequality?
Earth = heaven

Clear away injustice,
chuck out the adverts' images,
cancel the debts!
Earth = heaven!

Thank God!
It's A B C!

John Ll. Humphreys
Scotland/Wales

Imagine a World

Imagine a world where our leaders aren't liars,
    distorting reporting and spinning the news;
where all whistle-blowers and brave Jeremiahs
    are lauded, applauded and never abused.

Imagine a world where believers aren't fighting
    and shedding our blood in the name of their gods;
where faith is delightful, enlightening, inviting,
    and never deployed for crusades or jihads.

313

Imagine a world where the markets aren't idols,
    bowed down to and worshipped in envy and greed;
where wealth is released and the bankers are bridled,
    the poor have a plot and the famished a feed.

Imagine a world where there is no pollution,
    the air is so clear and the oceans are clean;
where humans don't threaten the earth's evolution,
    the animals flourish and forests are green.

Imagine a world as the Lord has intended,
    where goodness and justice and beauty preside;
a world we have broken that might yet be mended:
    the future is now, it is ours to decide.

Tune: The Bard of Armagh

Kim Fabricius
Wales/USA

Life in all its Fullness

I have come that you might have life – life in all its fullness.
(John 10.10 TEV)

Bless you Wise and Holy One
        for your down-to-earth
        vision of the best of
        what human life can be
Bless you WAHO
        for your call to life
        in all its fullness –
the more abundant life we live
        when we honour who we are
            as easily as we're enthralled by
            what others want us to be;
        when we're as eager
            to walk in another's shoes
            as we are to run off with them;

314

when we stop pursuing happiness
    and let it embrace us;
when we love
    not in the hope of getting
    but for the joy of giving;
when love is not
    what-you-can-do-for-me but
    what-we-can-be together;
when we can see
    not all the light is in ourselves
    not all the darkness in others;
when we choose our leaders
    not for their image
    but for their imagination
    not for the politics they play
    but for the principles they live;
when our society makes room
    for the individual
    and individuals make time
    for society;
when our economy thrives
    on our expressing who we are
    not on our spending what we have;
when we put as much stock
    in the loon as the loonie;
when we see the river as
    the blessing it is
    not the dammed thing
    we can make of it;
when the earth itself
    is our communion table;
when we're as awed by
    a cat's ingenuity
    as we are by
    computer technology;
when we bite into
    theology's questions

315

as readily as we swallow
technology's answers;
when we reject
that a long life is good enough
to accept
that a good life is long enough;
when we celebrate today
as not just all we have
but all we need;
when we see this more abundant life
not as our personal key
to the gates of heaven
but as the door to life
in all its fullness
Bless you Wise and Holy One
for calling us to life
in all its fullness
not just hereafter
but here and now.

Norm S. D. Esdon
Canada

The Everlasting Hope

A child born,
Wherever that is,
Whatever its name,
Gives all of us hope that
Maybe, just maybe
We could begin again.

A journey
Unknown, arduous or
With destination in sight,
Offers some hope
That our travel at times
May be light.

A flock, or the solitary wanderer
Lost, alone,
Have often been startled
At that hope that was to lead
Them home.

And stars,
When we think to glance,
Each reflect back
Our hope
To see beyond –
That chance.

A gift,
Precious, simple,
Offered to another –
One symbol of hope
That we remain
As sister, brother.

And so it is
That first story
Re-told re-lived,
That shall not pass,
Upon which all Hope and Life
Is cast.

Eve Jackson
England

Empty Beach

The beach was empty for them.
Sea was a far, thin, silver strip.
Apricot sky did pyrotechnic tricks,
Oh, miles above them,
And the wind went sshhh.

What is a sermon?
They faced into the theme?
Was it a meeting place
For the seen and the not seen?
Or opportunity to step from
The mundane through doors
Held open for others,
Between worlds,
Between different levels
Between mere words?

Perched on rose sandstone which
Old rollers had smashed smooth,
Sifting small pebbles,
They took on The Truth.
And all the way back
They were refining and defining
Along cool, even, evening pewter sand,
Miles beyond them.

Just before they called it a day,
The woman looked round to
Glimpse an horizon shining,
Then quickly turned away;
The man was making strides ahead.

As he spoke,
Beneath his right foot,
A pink shell,
Small as a newborn
Baby's thumbnail, broke.

Lucy Berry
England

318

Difference

I've seen your face so many times.
We often nod and smile.
I wonder what would happen
If we met, once, for a while.

You look so different to me.
I'm not at all like you.
I'm sure the details of our lives
Is hugely different too.

My age, my sex, the ones I love,
My accent and my skin
Are all the barriers we need.
So how could we begin?

My envy and my snobbishness
Could keep us worlds apart.
The fear that you won't like me
Makes it difficult to start.

I'd like to think that you're the same:
As different as me.
As big, small, young, old, black and white
As ever I will be.

And probably you really are
As weak, or toffee-nosed,
Or bleak, or brave, or selfless.
Or as open. Or as closed.

I wish that I could meet you
And begin that deep soul search.
It seems as though we might do
As we go to the same church.

Lucy Berry
England

Building Our Future Together

Prayer of Confession and Reconciliation

Leader: Let us be still and listen to the voice of God in our
             hearts.

Silence

People: – words of judgement that may have caused
             another pain,
             – compromises made that may have fragmented
             truth,
             – complacency that may have permitted hopeless-
             ness to replace hope in the heart of another,
             – apathy that may have stilled words and actions
             for justice in the lives of others.

Silence

Leader: let us confess that as a community there may have
             been times when

People: – we have failed to accept the stranger in our
             street,
             – we have not welcomed 'the other',
             – that one different to ourselves,
             – we have not offered a hand of acceptance and a
             smile of trust.

Silence

Leader: Let us confess that as a congregation there may
             have been times when

People: – we have not always been true to the teachings of
             Jesus of Nazareth,

       – we have not always walked in his footsteps and loved our neighbours as we love ourselves,

       – we have not practised the biblical gift of hospitality and have closed the door in the face of another.

Silence

People: O God forgive us and create in us a new heart to build communities founded on acceptance and tolerance. O God, forgive and fill us anew with your love so that we build a congregation that lives out the teachings of Jesus of Nazareth, our Risen Lord. Strengthen us to build a future together that embraces 'the other' and 'the stranger at our door' so that we live with gentleness and generosity, aware always of the needs of others, seeking always to put 'the other' first.

Leader: Hear these words of forgiveness and assurance:
In God there is new life.
Amen.

Passing the Peace

Leader: Listen to the words of Hebrews 13:1–3
(to be read by a member of the congregation)

Leader: In Passing the Peace today, let us remember God is in all people and all people are made in the image of God. When we refer to refugees, migrants and asylum seekers, we need to remember that they too are made in the image of God. Consequently in Passing the Peace we will take the hand of another or kiss on the cheek and say: 'I love the face of God I see in you.'

Prayers for All People

Leader: God of All Peoples, you call us to be at peace with our families, friends and neighbours.

People: **May we be a people of Peace.**

Leader: God of All Peoples, you call us to let mutual love continue.

People: **May we be a people of Love.**

Leader: God of All Peoples, you call us to show hospitality to strangers, for by doing so some have entertained angels without knowing it.

People: **May we be a people of Acceptance and Welcome.**

Leader: God of All Peoples help us to bring the light of the gospel to those traumatised and living in darkness, to understand and enter their pain as though we ourselves were in the same pain.

People: **May we be a people of Light.**

Leader: God of All Peoples, help us to bring hope to those living in despair and to remember those who are in detention as though we are in detention with them.

People: **May we be a people of Hope.**

Leader: God of All Peoples, help us to bring the gospel's peace to a divided world.
Jesus the same yesterday, today and forever.

People: **May we be a people of Peace.**

National Council of Churches
Australia

Epiphany

They came on camels
those Magi from the east
to find a Child
born King of the Jews.
Led by a star
they came to where he lay;
and Mary strangely inspired said
Stoop. Stoop down
and take him in your arms.
They stooped and held
the silent sleeping Child
and knew themselves possessed by love.
And knowing their belonging
they worshipped him
leaving gifts of gold
and frankincence and myrrh.
They journeyed home –
his presence in their hearts.

Harry Wiggett
South Africa

Praise to God, Creative Spirit

Praise to God, creative spirit,
Love made known in Christ, our Lord.
Genesis and revelation,
First and last, the living Word.
Who from atoms, mist and stardust
Shaped the order of the earth;
All its beauty, mystery, wonder,
Through the ages brought to birth.

We, the people of your likeness,
Though defaced by guilt and greed,

Still receive, by your great mercy,
Boundless riches for our need.
Still you call us to be partners
In the proving of your plan –
Place the bread and wine of blessing
In our dirty war-torn hands.

Shape our lives to hold compassion
For the suffering, shamed, and lost,
Seeking Christ in friend and stranger,
Without care for claim or cost.
Share the bitter blows of anger
Bear the searing scars of scorn –
Guard the coming generations –
Cherish children, yet unborn.

Where our greed deprives the hungry
Where our pride disdains the poor
Teach us how to share, unstinting,
All the wealth we hold in store.
Shame our arrogant obsession
With our own supremacy
Challenge us to live the Kingdom –
Justice, peace, integrity.

Recommended tune: Blaenwern

Jill Jenkins
England

Come Spirit

Come Spirit as light in darkness
Come Spirit as breath of life
Come Spirit cast your light
Come Spirit as strength and fortitude
Come Spirit ignite our passion

Come Spirit heal our pain
Come Spirit teach us justice
Come Spirit as hope in oppression
Come Spirit bless our brokenness

Catholic Women's Weekly
Australia

God of the Second Chance

Here we are, standing side by side,
Ready to sing and laugh and dance:
Happy that out of loneliness
God has arranged a second chance.

When lightning struck the steady oak,
Scorched stood the tree for year on year,
Till an unlooked-for miracle
Made tiny, tender leaves appear.

Nothing but bleak and barren sand
Showed in the desert. But dry roots,
Soaked up the loving, living rain,
Budded and blossomed and bore fruit.

So, we are healed and live again,
Learning again to love and cope.
Everyone joining in the joy.
Everyone sharing in the hope.

Thank you for loving us for life.
Thank you for your love-giving glance.
Thank you for rolling back the stone.
Thank you, God of the Second Chance.

Lucy Berry
England

Go in the Peace of Christ

Go in the peace of Christ.
Bring the light of God's love and hope
to displaced persons as you journey with them
On the road to freedom and a new life.

National Council of Churches
Australia

Moratorium on Magnificat

When Mary heard her cousin say
God's promises would be fulfilled
She looked towards the coming day
And sang a song to change the world.
This is the way the world will be
When God takes on humanity.

But while the poor support the proud
And tyrants thrive in lands and homes
And while the hungry people crowd
Around the mighty on their thrones:
While greed and need go on and on
How dare we think of Mary's song.

And when it comes to you and me
To show the world a God who cares,
We duck responsibility
And hide ourselves behind our prayers.
Till we have faced our common wrong
How dare we think of Mary's song.

Now face to face with Mary's Son,
Who healed the sick and took the blame,
We'll let God's promise call us on –
And then we'll never be the same.

Then we can sing with heart and voice,
In God my spirit does rejoice.

Tune: Sussex Carol

Janet Wootton
England

Anna
(Luke 2.36–38)

I must be over eighty now, I suppose.
I don't think much of the past anyway.
The world's been going to the dogs again.
I hardly leave the temple now. I pray
And fast. Then, when the evening comes,
I pop out into town and buy a snack
And nip back here to eat it,
Out of the way, right at the back.

I don't need much to eat. I barely sleep.
I like to watch the temple people and
Folk up from the country, and the sacrifice;
The meaty, smoky smell of fat burning.
They give me some sometimes, which is nice.

At night in my corner, I worry about the world.
The floor is hard. I get a little cold.
But I love my temple. I love to live with God.
And I like to get the news from women
Who come in. This is my home,
Full of good hustle and bustle.
And the priests kindly leave me alone
And call me a prophet. And I can make sense.

When the special baby came the other day,
Simeon grabbed Him and started with poems.

I went to my place and said:
'Thank you God. Thank you God. Thank you God.
Thank you, my dear Lord on High.'

And then I told everyone . . . Everyone!
I will gossip the lovely news until the day I die.

Lucy Berry
England

Mary, Mother

Mary was a beautiful woman
in loveliness of character,
shy, intelligent and deeply spiritual.
She did not look for greatness
but when God called her
she was ready to obey and serve.
As the messenger of God told her,
she was to be the mother
of a special child
who would grow in years and wisdom
and become the Saviour of the world.
Hers was the humility and the obedience,
the greatness and the glory,
the pride and the depth of suffering.

John Johansen-Berg
England

According to Mary

It was only weeks
since I'd taken my alabaster jar
of ointment, washed his feet
at the house of the Pharisee.
Now he hung on the cross;
This time the Valerian
did not touch him.

When we got him down
I wanted to cleanse the clotted roses
from his head,
claw the thorns from his flesh,
but my tears would not wash
nor my hair wipe away his blood.

In the garden
when next we met, he allowed me
to kiss him, to bind his healing hands
with myrtle. He placed a sheaf of
marigolds on my breast –
said he would send an angel
to guide me to a cave.

Where I would live, lifted up
each day to glimpse heaven,
worshipping him always
with my eyes and hair.

Denise Bennett
England

The Lonely Road

They said his face looked
like granite
as he turned away,

329

set his path for Jerusalem
and certain death.

Granite! Who knows what
lay beneath that hardness,
what suffering of soul.
We cannot know,
only guess and wonder
that he would willingly
do this for us.

Along the lonely road
he walked.
Weary at times, determined.
So much at stake,
too much for one person,
to bear.

Looking back two thousand years,
we give thanks
for others who chose to walk
with him.
Offering companionship,
a listening ear, smiles, a hug maybe,
food and drink.
Sensitive to his need to be alone.

We honour Mary
who looked beneath the surface.
Seeing his anguish
she took her precious perfume
anointing him for death.
A simple act which so touched him,
he said she would be remembered
whenever the Good News is preached.

Another Mary overturned the demands
of hospitality and gave instead

an attentive ear,
tuned to his thoughts and words.
Food and fuss could come later.

We remember the many
suffering for the sake of peace
who have trodden the lonely road.
With gratitude, we acknowledge
those who, today, struggle
to put flesh on his words,
'The Kingdom of God is near,
so act justly, love mercy and
walk humbly with your God.'

We pray we may have courage
to walk the same road.
All of us, a great cloud of witnesses,
following behind,
the One who first loved us
and proved that love
by walking the lonely road.

Wendy d Ward
Aotearoa New Zealand

Useful Contact Information

Asian Women's Resource Centre for Culture and Theology
119C–2 Batu 3½
Jalan Kelang Lama
58000 Kuala Lumpur
Malaysia

CAFOD
2 Romero Close
Stockwell Road
London
SW9
Tel: 0207 733 7900
www.cafod.org.uk

Christian Aid
35 – 41 Lower Marsh
London
SE1 9RT
Tel: 0207 620 4444

Council for World Mission
a32/34 Great Peter Street
London
SW1P 2DB
Tel: 0207 222 4214

Fathers Figure is a book from the project (correct title)
Father Figures (correct name of the project)
Sheffield
Contact Michael Watson
Tel: 0114 249 5981

Leprosy Mission
Goldhay Way
Orton Goldhay
Peterborough
PE2 5GZ
Tel: 01733 370505

Traidcraft
Kingsway
Gateshead
Tyne and Wear
NE11 0NE
Tel: 0845 2309702

Index of Authors

Index of Titles

Chapter Two

Chapter Three

Chapter Four

Chapter Five

Chapter Six

Chapter Seven

Acknowledgements and Sources

Chapter One

Alem © Sarah Ingle
Angel on Call © Wendy Whitehead

Beware Hasty Assumptions © Wendy Whitehead
Beyond © John Ll. Humphreys
Blessed Are . . . © Jane Deren, Marissa Maurer and Julie Viera in *Catholic Social Teaching and Human Rights: An Educational Packet for the Center of Concern*, Washington DC, April 1998
Bless the Lord for Your Coming © Duncan L. Tuck

Call No One Stranger © Patricia Mulhall Sr/CAFOD
Celebrate Each Difference © Andrew Pratt

Doors © Harry Wiggett
Drive out the Prejudices © Raymond Chapman from *Following the Gospel through the Year*, The Canterbury Press

Each Person Is God's Image © Per Harling
Emmaus Walk © Ann Lewin
Entertaining an Angel Unawares © Susan Hardwick
Exchange © Adam from *Fathers Figure*, an anthology of writing by fathers in Sheffield

From the Unborn Child to His Father © Dave from *Fathers Figure*, an anthology of writing by fathers in Sheffield

Here Was a Man © Eve Jackson

I Vow to Love My Neighbour © Andrew Pratt
Is it Nothing to You? © Gillian Collins
Incomer © Margot Arthurton
Inn Signs © Ann Lewin
Invitation, The © Claire Smith

Jesus, Friend and Brother © Tony Singleton/CAFOD

Let the Little Children © Janet Lees
Let's Have a Meal, Let's Have a Feast © Kim Fabricius
Lift up the Other, A Sister from the African Continent
Little Flute © Lucy Berry
Love Is Made the Way You Want it to Be © Zola F.
Loving a Neighbour © Salvador T. Martinez
Loving God © Marjorie Dobson

Meeting and Eating © Janet Lees
Mistaken Identity © Wendy Ross-Barker
Move Out – To Entertain © Geoffrey Duncan
My Church – A Bridge for the Stranger © Geoffrey Duncan

On Being an Angel © Aled Edwards
Open Door © John Johansen-Berg

Reaching Out © Jayne Greathead
Receiving Jesus © Anne Richards
Responding to Small Miracles © Duncan L. Tuck
Ruth (1) © Marjorie Dobson

Sheltering God © Jane Deren, Marissa Maurer and Julie Viera in *Catholic Social Teaching and Human Rights: An Educational Packet for the Center of Concern*, Washington DC, April 1998
Single Prayer, The © Eve Jackson
Solitude by Marjorie Dobson from *Mulit-coloured Maize* reproduced by permission of Stainer and Bell Ltd
Souvenir © Denise Bennett
Strangers and Angels © Heather Johnston

They Came to Tea © Geoffrey Duncan
Torn © Margot Arthurton
Welcome Stranger © Susan Hardwick

You Are Welcome © Duncan L. Tuck
Yusuf, Yitzak and John © Harry Wiggett

Chapter Two

Acts of God – Reflection on Rights, A © John Proctor
African Hand-Carved Table © Geoffrey Herbert
AIDS © Salvador T. Martinez

Bed and Breakfast © Ann Lewin

Christmas Card © Ann Lewin

Deir Yassin © Patricia Price-Tomes

Fresh Water is a First © Fiona Thomson/Traidcraft

God of Mercy and of Grace © J Jayakiran Sebastian
Golan Water © Patricia Price-Tomes

Holy Spirit Breathe Your Comfort © Per Harling
Humble Cup of Tea, The © Fiona Thomson/Traidcraft

I am Wonderfully Made © Hope Antone from *In God's Image*, Vol. 20, No.
3 September 2001
I'm not Just a Back © Jayne Greathead
In God's Agenda © Samuel Pachuau
Inside Out © Margot Arthurton

Kapasule © Fiona Ritchie Walker

Let Justice Flow © Susan Hardwick
Let the World be Changed © Garth Hewitt
Lord of Justice and Peace © Miguel Laburu, Fr
Love Kindness © Andrew Pratt

Malawi Prayers © Fiona Thomson/Traidcraft
Malaysian Woman, A, A Malaysian Woman from *In God's Image*, Vol. 21,
No. 3 September 2002
Move Towards Justice for All People © Geoffrey Duncan
My Mother in Heaven © Wong Mei Yuk from *In God's Image*, Vol. 19 No.3,
September 2000

News from Africa © Cecily Taylor
Not Alone © Brian Louis Pearce

Our Global Village © John Johansen-Berg

People of the West, The © Garth Hewitt
Poppy Is Her Name © Helene McLeod
Power Games © Ann Lewin
Prayer for Charity and a Preferential Option for the Poor © Mary Lou
Kownacki OSB
Prayer for Human Rights Day, A © Christian Conference of Asia

345

Prayer for the Tea Chain © Fiona Thomson/Traidcraft
Prayers of the People, The © Primate's World Relief and Development
Fund, Anglican Church of Canada

Ragged Child © Margot Arthurton
Rock-crusher © Bernard Thorogood

Sealed in Concrete © Andrew Ashdown
Silent People, The © Stainer and Bell Ltd
Standing Near the Cross ... © Jean Mortimer
Stranger in Our Midst © Norm S. D. Esdon
Suffer Little Children ... © Susan Hardwick

Temple Cleansing © Ann Lewin
There Is Much I Would Do © Duncan L. Tuck
Trouble with an Asylum Seeker, The © John Proctor

Why Them? © Ann Lewin
Witnesses © John Johansen-Berg
Woman You Are Called ... © Bibiana Bunuan from *In God's Image*, Vol. 21,
No. 2 June 2002
You'll Find Me © Brian Louis Pearce

Chapter Three

Asylum Seekers © Ann Lewin
At Worship © Bernard Thorogood

... but Understand © Eve Jackson

Cover Us With Your Wings, O Lord © Margaret McNulty/CAFOD

Dog Roses © Denise Bennett

God Sees, God Suffers © Lynne Chitty
God of Compassion © Helen Coleman
Goodbye England © Anthea Dove

Happy Birthday, Baby Jesus © Kim Fabricius
He Broke the Rules © Garth Hewitt
Holy and Liberating God © National Council of Churches, Australia
Homeless in Egypt © John Johansen-Berg
Humane © Wendy d Ward

Kind Thought for Asylum Seekers, A, Anonymous

Lament for an Olive Grove © Patricia Price-Tomes
Litany of Commitment for Human Rights Day © Presbyterian Peace Program/USA
Lord, Clear Our Eyes © National Council of Churches, Australia
Lord, No One Is a Stranger to You © CAFOD England

Marianne © Lucy Berry
Missed Childhood © Ann Lewin
My Friend © Bernard Thorogood

No Cot for the Future © Derek Webster
No Place of Safety © Jean Mortimer
Not so this Christmas © Wendy Ross-Barker

On the Timor Sea © Bernard Thorogood
Orchard, The © Janet Lees
Our Only Salvation © Norm S D Esdon

Pattern of Strangers, The © Duncan L. Tuck
Portable Things © Lucy Berry
Praying with those who Weep © Wendy Ross-Barker
Protecting the Persecuted © National Council of Churches, Australia

Rainbow World © Susan Hardwick
Reconciliation: Reality © Eve Jackson
Refugee and/or Migrant Sunday © John Murphy, Fr
Refugee, The © Zola F
Refugees (1) © Ann Lewin
Refugees (2) © South African Catholic Bishop's Conference/CAFOD England
River of Hope, The © National Council of Churches, Australia
Ruth (2) © Lucy Berry

Seen in Ramallah © Patricia Price-Tomes
Singing, Praying and Holding Olive Branches © Andrew Ashdown and Susan Sayers
Stations of the Cross in the Gulag © Derek Webster
Strangers in a Strange Land © Steve de Gruchy

To Nurture Conflict – A Recipe © Patricia Price-Tomes
Twenty-First-Century Nativity © Patricia Price-Tomes

walking wounded © Naomi Young

347

Chapter Four

Accepting who 'I Am', Anonymous
At Eighty One © Denise Bennett

Bless all who Come in Anger © Lynne Chitty
Blue Tulips © Elizabeth Cambridge
Boxes © Naomi Young

Depression © Christine Ractliff
Despised – Rejected – Crucified © Norm S. D. Esdon

Edelweiss © Denise Bennett
Exile of a Gay Man © Geoffrey Herbert

From the Other Side © Dorothy Stewart

Gay Child Speaks, Lucy Berry © British Broadcasting Corporation. Used with permission
Get on with It © Andrew Pratt
Glass in the Dustbin, The © Kelvin Harris
God Search © Colin Ferguson

Home © Lucy Berry

Keeping Faith © Denise Bennett
Known by Name © Ann Lewin

Let Her Go Hungry © Sarah Ingle
Life's Lesson © Nia Rhosier
Like a Child © Eve Jackson
Lord of This Day © Corrymeela Community
Lydia © Geoffrey Herbert

Mobility Allowance © Geoffrey Herbert

Nathanael © Geoffrey Herbert
Not that Easy © Jayne Greathead
Not the Last Word © Ann Lewin

On the Edge © Wendy Ross-Barker

Pray for Me © Anne Sardeson

Chapter Five

Kingdom Has Come Close, The © Geoffrey Herbert
Kiss in Waitrose, A © Colin Ferguson

Let's Call Her Jackie © Rosemary Watts
Litany of Blessing and Anointing, A © Jean Mortimer

Mary's Psalm © Derek Webster

1.30pm HMP Holloway © Lucy Berry reproduced by permission of the
Governor, HMP Holloway, London UK
Other End of the Street, The © Patricia Price-Tomes
Our Hospital, Our Garden © Roger Grainger

Passion of the Christ, The © John Ll. Humphreys
Potatoes © Colin Ferguson
Playtime of Terror © John Johansen-Berg
Prayer for Prison Chaplains, A © Susan Hardwick
Preaching to the Confused © Barbara Moss
Prison of Prejudice, The © John Johansen-Berg
Prisoner, The © Susan Hardwick
Public Has Forgotten Them, The © Rosemary Watts

Reading Between the Lines © Jean Mortimer
Release © Bernard Thorogood
Release of Prisoners © John Johansen-Berg

Shadow in the Middle, The © Garth Hewitt
Silent Prisoner, The © Harry Wiggett
Superwoman © Lucy Berry
Survivor © Patricia Price-Tomes

Three Mothers for Peace © John Johansen-Berg

We Come Together in Freedom © Lynne Chitty
Welcome, Mordechai © John Johansen-Berg

Yo Creo en Nicaragua (I Believe in Nicaragua) © Garth Hewitt

Chapter Six

Angela's Story © Leprosy Mission, The

Blessed are the Poor © Geoffrey Herbert

Christian Communication, Anonymous
Come In, Angel © Bernard Thorogood

Denial of Christ, The – from Whom Do We Deny Wholeness? © Christine
Cargill from *In God's Image*, Vol. 20, No. 4, December 2001
Dis-illusioned © Zola F.
Disturb Me © Lynne Chitty

Face to Face © Wendy Whitehead

have you ever? © Naomi Young
Hold Us Safe in Your Love © Roger Shaljean

Jesus Talked with Gentiles © Kim Fabricius

Least of These, The © Claire Smith
Left Alone © Frances Ballantyne
Let us Pray in the Words of the Psalmist © Deenabandhu Manchala

Magdalene's Business © Lucy Berry
Margaret of Cortona © Brian Louis Pearce
Migrant © Salvador T. Martinez
Minister Reaches Out © Council for World Mission/Geoffrey Duncan

Note from God © Denise Bennett

Only God to Call On © Lucy Berry
Outcast © Susan Hardwick
Outcast, The © John Johansen-Berg

Saint of the Streets, A © Padraig Regan, Fr
See, the Man © Geoffrey Herbert
Steadfast Love, Justice and Righteousness © Claire Smith
Street Nightingales © Jean Mortimer
Stretch Out Your Hand © Wendy Whitehead

Take Our Disorientation © Per Harling
This Is Christmas © Jessica Isherwood
This Is Real © Eve Jackson
Together We're Stronger © Leprosy Mission, The

We Confess Our Failings in Community © Corrymeela Community
What a Prospect! © John Johansen-Berg
Who? © Margot Arthurton

Who's that? © Janet Lees
Who Will Speak if We Don't? © National Council of Churches, Australia
Woman of the Streets, A © Lynne Chitty

You May Cry © Per Harling

Chapter Seven

According to Mary © Denise Bennett
Anna © Lucy Berry

Building Our Future Together © National Council of Churches, Australia

Church Is not Confined by Boundaries, The © Ana and Tod Gobledale
Come Spirit © *Catholic Women's Weekly*, Australia
Creed, A © CAFOD England

Difference © Lucy Berry

Earth = Heaven © John Ll. Humphreys
Empowering God, Dynamic Christ © Christine E. Collin
Empty Beach © Lucy Berry
Entertaining Angels © Zola F.
Epiphany © Harry Wiggett
Everlasting Hope, The © Eve Jackson
Exciting God © Marjorie Dobson

Go in the Peace of Christ © National Council of Churches, Australia
God Is Really Wonderful © Wendy Ross-Barker
God of the Second Chance © Lucy Berry

Hill of Harmony © Nia Rhosier
How Odd of God © John Proctor

Imagine © Naomi Young
Imagine a World © Kim Fabricius
In a Quiet Way © Eve Jackson

Just Imagine © Eve Jackson

Life in All it's Fullness © Norm S. D. Esdon
Lonely Lord's Prayer, The © Duncan L. Tuck
Lonely Road, The © Wendy d Ward

Love Is a Key in Lock © Lucy Berry
Lover's Response, The © Zola F.

Mary, Mother © John Johansen-Berg
Meditation on The Lord's Prayer © Group of Refugees, El Salvador
Misfit © Barnard Thorogood
Moratorium on Magnificat © Janet Wootton

New Heaven on Earth, A © Susan Hardwick

One Candle © Marjorie Dobson

Praise to God, Creative Spirit © Jill Jenkins
Prayer for the Church, A © Norm S. D. Esdon

Rainbow Promise © John Johansen-Berg
Resolutions for the Twenty-First Century © Doreen Gazey

Sparrows © Geoffrey Herbert

Waiting Time, The © Jill Jenkins
We Are All God's Children © Pearl Willemssen Hoffman
West-Eastern Diwan Orchestra © John Swarbrick

Yasmin's Rose © Patricia Price-Tomes
You Made the Earth © Linda Jones/CAFOD